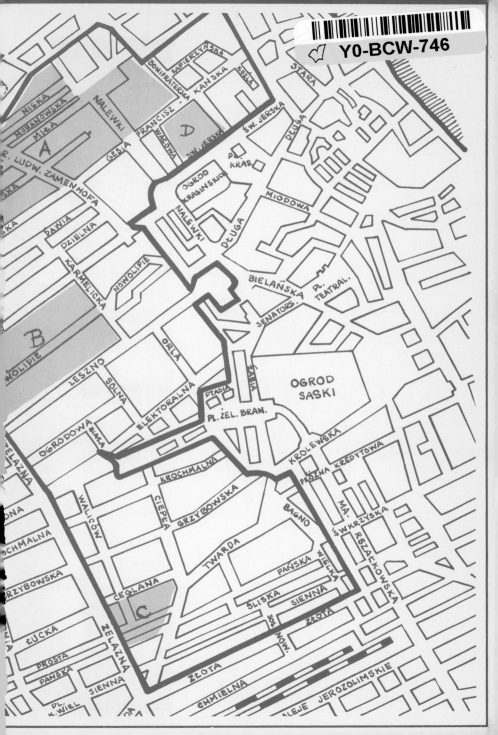

TO DIE WITH HONOR

TO DIE WITH HONOR

⮜§The Uprising of the Jews
in the Warsaw Ghetto §⮞

by LEONARD TUSHNET

THE CITADEL PRESS   NEW YORK

FIRST EDITION

Copyright © 1965 by Leonard Tushnet. All rights reserved. Published by The Citadel Press, 222 Park Avenue South, New York, N. Y. 10003. Manufactured in the United States of America by The Haddon Craftsmen, Inc., Scranton, Pa. Published simultaneously in Canada by George J. McLeod Ltd.

Library of Congress Catalog Card No.: 65-15488

To the Memory of My Father, Samuel

Acknowledgments

The author wishes to thank Miss Dina Abramowicz of the YIVO Institute for Jewish Research and the staff of the Maplewood (N.J.) Public Library for their advice and help in the preparation of this book.

CONTENTS

Foreword

More than twenty years have passed since the uprising of the Jews in the Ghetto of Warsaw—an event unique in the history of the Jews and of the world. Every happening in history is unique it is true, yet some are more unique than others. Valley Forge, Thermopylae, Napoleon in retreat from Moscow, Joan of Arc at Orleans—all stand out as historic, rather than historical, events, firing us with their dramatic impact.

Such was the Jewish Resistance in Warsaw, reaching its climax in April, 1943. Against it was arrayed an implacable enemy, with every psychological and military weapon at its disposal, with a precise and coldly planned program for total extermination of the Jews. The resistance movement in the Ghetto was almost completely isolated from the rest of Warsaw. Its members were weak, virtually weaponless. They were certain of their ultimate defeat and yet they fought. Sustained neither by the hope of Paradise nor the glories that await martyrs in heaven, they stood their ground. Survivors of a three-year attempt to kill them by starvation, by disease, by cremation, a remnant saved from burning by caprice and chance, divided in ideology, ragged would-be soldiers unlearned in the arts of warfare, they were stubborn in their resistance and gave battle for honor, for vengeance, for a brave new world. Glory to their memory!

Except for several sections of larger works, the full ac-

count of the Jewish Resistance in Warsaw is not available
to the English-reading public. I have (to use an Irish
phrase) a *geas* upon me to give such an account. This book
is in answer to that compulsion. I have drawn upon many
sources and secondary writings to do so, (some noted in the
appended bibliography). I have tried to simplify in its
telling a complex situation.

To write such a history, as Pirenne said he tried to
with the history of Belgium, "as though it were the history
of the Etruscans," is beyond my powers. But I have tried.
To do so, I found it necessary to omit any extended dis-
cussion of the political ramifications of the resistance movement, to avoid judgments on the merits of the roles played
by individuals, groups and parties, and to give but the
barest outline of the inception of the resistance. I have also
foregone any detailed description of the parts played by
the German authorities or the Polish organizations active
at the time, except where such a description is necessary
for a fuller understanding of the measures taken by the
Jews. I have also, in the interest of carrying the action forward, suppressed my natural desire to give complete biog-
raphies of the major protagonists and to mention the names
of every one of the fighters. And finally, the most difficult
task of all, I have tried to avoid dwelling on the many
pathetic, romantic, even picturesque, incidents in order to
give a straight factual narrative.

Where necessary, for easier reading, I have anglicized
Polish and Yiddish names. Footnotes have been omitted;
a glossary is given at the end of the book.

TO DIE WITH HONOR

CHAPTER I

Before November, 1940

THE German victory over Poland and the succeeding pogroms, racial laws, and discriminatory activities of the occupation forces culminated in the segregation of the Warsaw Jews in a walled ghetto in November, 1940. Up to that time, with few exceptions, Jewish opinions about the future were as varied as those of the pre-war period, and Jewish disunity persisted. There was a nonpolitical mass, a religious group, and three well-organized political factions. Of the last, the Bund was the largest and most influential, closely followed by the Zionist parties, themselves divided, and farther behind, by the Communists. Each organization had its own publications and its own band of devoted followers, and each called on its sympathizers to carry on, *mutatis mutandis*, under the Germans as they had under the Polish government.

The Bund regarded the German occupiers in the same light as the pre-war semi-Fascist anti-proletarian Polish reactionaries, the former only being more viciously exaggerated in their malice than the latter. In line with that attitude, its political activity against the Germans varied only in degree from that previously undertaken against the Polish regime. Illegal papers were distributed. Relief committees were organized to alleviate the distress of the refugees and the homeless. An illegal trade union commission was set up to rebuild the workers' syndicates in co-ordination with the (also illegal) Polish trade union movement. An underground political committee had the function of initiating and carrying on anti-Fascist actions.

The Zionists, united in nationalist hopes but separated in political approach, also had relief committees and propaganda sections. The Nazis, to them, were but the boldest expression of the anti-Semitism of the nations; hope for the Jews lay only in a Jewish state in Palestine. To this end they trained their young people and combatted the internationalism of the Bundists. They stressed, from the religious or secular sides, depending on their viewpoint, the necessity for preservation of Jewish ideas and for emigration to Palestine. They published in August, 1940, for example, a 99-page anthology of historical and literary material describing the persecutions of the Jews from the time of the Crusades through the Ukrainian pogroms of 1917-1920 to demonstrate that the Jewish people had survived other trials and tribulations. The Revisionists, the extreme right wing, printed (a Herculean task, considering the situation in Warsaw) in the same month a memorial to Vladimir Jabotinsky, the founder of their movement, using it as a springboard for denunciation of those who thought Jews could lead a full life in exile.

The Communists, in conformity with their theory that the Jews were an integral part of general Polish society, had no special Jewish branches other than those based purely on location in Jewish sections of the city. The Friends of the Soviet Union and the Hammer-and-Sickle Society had several such clubs on that basis, as had the youth group, Spartacus. Even more internationalist than the Bund and yet more Polish-nationalist, the Communists took Poles into these Jewish groups and used Polish in their publications, although the Jewish Spartacus section put out a hectographed bulletin, *Baginen,* in Yiddish. The Communist posters used familiar slogans: "Down with Imperialism!" "Down with Fascism!" "German Fascism means the destruction of mankind!" On the more practical side, they called for acts of sabotage against the Germans and succeeded in combining with some of the Left Zionist groups for specific measures along that line.

By far the greatest mass of the Jews, cursed with a sense of history, looked on German rule as another grievous burden to be borne. There was a shrug, and then the shoulders bent a little more, the heads bowed a little more, and they submitted.

CHAPTER II

November, 1940, to January, 1942

THE organized groups viewed the institution of the closed ghetto as a call to intensify their activities and to particularize them.

The underground press took on new vigor despite the increased hardships of publication and distribution. The papers, clandestinely mimeographed, were given out under cover of darkness. Their numbers were limited: the Bund organs, for instance, came out in 300 to 500 copies per issue, but there were at least twenty readers of each copy. The journals, no matter what their political origin, had common aims: to combat apathy, to give hope for eventual liberation, to build morale and to fight the pernicious diligence with which the *Judenrat* (the governing council of Jews appointed by the Nazis) and the Jewish police carried out German orders. Active resistance was not called for; passive resistance by avoidance of regulations was advised.

There were as many publications as there were parties —more, actually, because some parties had two or three, and nonpolitical groups occasionally put out papers. The most widely read papers were those of the Bund, especially the monthly *Za Naszą i Waszą Wolność* ("For Our and Your Freedom") and the weeklies *Der Vekker* ("The Awakener") and the *Yugent Shtimme* ("Voice of Youth"), the latter the organ of *Zukunft*, the Socialist youth group. In November, 1940, *Zukunft* put out a bulletin whose cover showed the walls of the Ghetto being smashed by clasped hands from each side of the wall, with the slogan, "Long live the brotherhood of nations!" That theme was to be the burden, in a double sense, of the whole Bund program. The Bund also published a *Bulletin* (in Polish and Yiddish), *Tsait-fragn* ("Current Questions"), and *Nowa Młodzież* ("New Youth").

Every Zionist faction had its paper, coming out more or less irregularly. Left Poale Zion had *Proletarisher Gedank* ("Proletarian Thought"), *Yugent Ruf* ("Call of Youth"), *Avant-garde*, and *Nasze Hasło* ("Our Slogan"). Hashomer Hatzair had *Przed Wiośnie* ("The Eve of Spring"), *Jutrznia* ("Dawn"), and the weekly *Oifbruz* ("Ferment"). Dror published twenty numbers of its journal, "Notes," in Yiddish and ten in Polish—a weekly estimated to have been read by 3000 Ghetto dwellers. Poale Zion (Socialist-Zionists) published *Bafreiung* ("Liberation") and an inner-party organ in Polish as well. The youth division of the General Zionists had their *Shaviv* ("The Spark," in Hebrew), and the parent group, *Unzer Hoffnung* ("Our Hope").

The Communists put out a weekly, *Morgen Frei*, later to become a daily bulletin under the name of *Morgen Freiheit* ("Morning Freedom"), in addition to the irregularly issued *Proletarishes Radio-Bulletin*, based on foreign radio reports. The Communists in this period, like the other

parties, pursued their own *idée fixe*. *Morgan Freiheit* saw in
the establishment of the Ghetto fear on the part of the
Germans that the Jews and the Poles would unite against
their oppressors, and therefore the Nazis wanted to separate
the Jewish working class from its Polish counterpart.

Even splinter groups put out papers. The Trotskyites had
Przegląd Marksistowski ("Marxist Review"); the assimila-
tionists, *"Zhagiev"* ("The Torch"); and Jewish members of
the Polish Socialist Party (not to be confused with Bundists), their *Ghetto Podziemne* ("Ghetto Underground").

The press did indeed mobilize the populace to action.
Through its efforts, attempts were made to force the *Judenrat* to divide the limited food supply more equitably, to
increase relief to the refugees, to curb the luxury living of
the rich. In March, 1941, attacks were made on the caba-
rets and restaurants frequented by the wealthy. In April
and May, and again in September, demonstrations were
organized against the *Judenrat's* co-operation with the
Germans in providing workers for the slave-labor camps.
Against the Germans the most dramatic result of the passive resistance movement was the fur collection sabotage in
December, 1941; instead of turning their fur coats and fur
pieces over to the Nazis, the Jews burned them or so
mangled them that they were worthless. The Nazi collector
bewailed his inability to reach even the minimum quota
assigned to him.

But all the agitation and the morale-building was only
a cover-up for the failure of the parties to decide on a
definite course of action, on a goal to be achieved. The
youth groups were hot for active resistance and revenge,
but were held back by their elders, influential for their past

revolutionary deeds and powerful by their present control of organizational funds and apparatus. The Left was convinced that German Fascism was inevitably doomed; therefore, the Jews should sit tight until Hitler's downfall. The Zionists counted on support from world Jewry. The religious said prayers—especially the mourner's *Kaddish*. Meanwhile, hunger and typhus and casual brutality took their toll of the Ghetto population.

The attack on the Soviet Union by the Nazis brought new hope to the Ghetto and a revived desire for active resistance. The young Zionists mobilized first; Hechalutz set up fighting units. They reasoned: The Russians will obviously soon throw back the Germans, and in their retreat the German Army will undoubtedly try to make pogroms; resistance would not only save the Jews but would also undermine German strength. Most of the inhabitants of the Ghetto did not go so far in their thinking; they enthusiastically but passively awaited liberation by the advancing Red Army. Their hopeful anticipation made them irrational; the news of Russian defeats was taken as Nazi bluff. They sang:

> *Żydzi, nie bójcie się!*   Jews fear nothing!
> *Polacy, radujcie się!*   Poles, rejoice!
> *Niemcy, pakujcie się!*   Germans, get going!

The news of the extermination of the Jews of Vilna and of other provincial cities brought a cold chill to the Ghetto. Hope began to fade once more. They still believed that the Germans would be defeated, but when?—too late for the Jews? The advocates of active resistance found more listeners now. That resistance was not hopeless was proved by the Jews of Novogrodek in Byelorussia, where the Germans were fought long enough to allow most of the inhabitants to escape to the forests. That it was possible, even in the Ghetto, was demonstrated by the 162 cases of individual attacks on police the week of September 22, 1941, going up to 185 and 194 in the following two weeks, and by the increase of passive resistance and sabotage. The workers in a clothing factory, for example, sent out military uniforms with trousers sewn together, misplaced buttons, reversed sleeves, and pockets upside down.

The mass unrest, increased also by the ever-advancing mortality from starvation, had its effect on the leaders of the Jewish community. Many meetings were held, without result as far as support for active resistance went. There were those who were profiting by the general misery; they were content with things as they were. There were others, opportunists who placed self-survival first, who counselled against hasty action. There were idealists also, who, out of lofty motives, advised against active resistance. Such a one was Orzech, a Bundist, who said, "Let us fight—but only when the Poles fight too. . . . This is only one war—the war of the oppressed against the oppressors. . . . Poles, as well as Jews, are murdered daily. When the proper time comes, Jewish and Polish workers will rise and fight side by side!" Another was Doctor Ignatz Schipper, an intellectual of great weight in Jewish circles, a former deputy to the Sejm, who argued that for the Jews to declare war on the Germans would mean the extermination of the entire Ghetto, that now was the time for submission, even for sacrificing a few for the many. Another was Rabbi Zishe Friedman, who said violence was not the way of the Jews, merciful children of the merciful. Others pointed out that the Germans would apply the principle of collective responsibility, and the death of hundreds would be caused by one rash act of protest. Others said Warsaw was not Vilna, that the Germans would not treat the Jews in the very heart of Europe the same way they treated those in the Soviet Union. And still others calmly pointed out the ridiculousness of armed conflict with neither arms nor trained fighters.

Even among the supporters of armed resistance there was no agreement. The Spartacus group held heated debates: should they leave the Ghetto to join the partisans (guerrilla bands) in the woods surrounding Warsaw, where weapons were more easily obtainable and where reprisals on innocent Jews would be avoided, or should they stay in the Ghetto to harass the Germans and protect the Jewish inhabitants from the *Judenrat* and the Gestapo hangers-on? Hashomer Hatzair and youth divisions of other Zionist parties had the same problem. A compromise was made—some left for the woods, some stayed behind as cadres for the hoped-for fighting organization.

A Jewish fighting force remained a dream for the time being. Organizational unity was a necessity, not only a desideratum, but some groups regarded others as wild-eyed radicals, or as self-servers, or as glory-seekers, or as possible Gestapo informers. Each group felt secure in its own shell, safe in the knowledge that its own comrades were trustworthy.

CHAPTER III

January to July, 1942

ARLY in 1942, a rumor spread throughout underground circles and thence to the entire Ghetto that a Soviet parachutist had landed in the Ghetto for the specific purpose of aiding the Jews. The Jewish masses, already looking for help from astrologers, fortune tellers, and Kabbalists, gave wide credence to the tale; it supported their desire to feel that they had not been forgotten by the whole world, that someone was still interested in them.

The parachutist was Pinya Kartin, better known by his party name, Andrzej Schmidt. A chemist by profession, an ex-officer of the International Brigade in Spain under the name of Jaroslav Dombrowski, he had entered the Ghetto, not by parachute, but by the more prosaic method of bribing a wall-guard. He came as an official representative of the *Polska Partja Robotnicza* (P.P.R.), which was the new name of the former Polish Communist Party, now expanded to include Left Socialists, Constitutionalists, and unaffiliated patriotic Poles. Aid to the Jews was one of the planks in the P.P.R. platform; another was aid to the Soviet Union in its war against Germany; another was an independent Socialist Poland. A Jewish brigade would be helpful in all of these aims; so would Jewish partisans; so would sabotage and general disorder in the occupied areas.

The *Morgen Freiheit* of March 10th called for immediate efforts to organize a national (Polish) uprising, to restore citizenship rights to the Jews, to break down the Ghettos, to rebuild a new, more democratic Poland. An editorial statement declared that the P.P.R. would become a national front against Hitler Fascism, uniting all forces in one uprising against the Nazis. With this issue the *Morgen Freiheit* ceased to exist. Its place was taken by a number of smaller P.P.R. publications—*Einigkeit* ("Unity"), *Hammer*, and *Zum Kamf* ("To Battle"), edited by Joseph Lewartowski (Ghetto pseudonym: Finkelstein), the former head of the Jewish Bureau of the Central Committee of the Polish Communist Party.

The P.P.R. committee (consisting of Lewartowski, Schmidt, and Samuel Zimmerman) met regularly and secretly in the apartment of Dora Blatman, at 10 Ogrodowa Street. Their first task was to reorganize and link together the loose left-wing groups already existing in the Ghetto: Spartacus, Lithuanian Social Democrats, Communists. Conspiratorial techniques were taught and recruits gained for the coming battle with the Germans. Meanwhile, sabotage and slow-down tactics were encouraged. Spartacus set up a library at 53 Nowolipie Street and hid there a collection of German uniforms to be used later in the presumably soon-forthcoming guerrilla actions. It conducted discussions on military organization and on how to counter the anti-Soviet orientation of the Bund.

For the Bund and the Zionists were active now, too. The

Bund put out additional publications: *Dos Freie Wort*
("The Free Word"), *Der Glok* ("The Bell"), *Der Shturm*
("The Storm"), *Oif der Vach* ("On Guard"). The publications, it was charged by Dr. Leon Feiner, the leader of
the opposition in the Bund, served but to cover up the do-
nothing tactics and to further the ambitions of the clique in
leadership. The Revisionists went one step further than
propaganda. In April, Dr. David Wdowinski went with a
committee to Dr. Ignatz Schipper to propose the formation
of a Jewish Self Defense. Dr. Schipper laughed off the
proposal: "You Revisionists are always hotheads." He said
that it was physically impossible to wipe out a ghetto of
almost half a million people, that the Germans would not
dare to flout world public opinion by such an act, and that
Czerniakow, the Chairman of the *Judenrat*, had been assured that there would be three permanent ghettos in
Poland (Warsaw, Radom, Krakow).

The Zionists, on the initiative of Poale Zion, through the
Hechalutz leaders, called a conference in March to which
came representatives of Poale Zion, Left Poale Zion, the
Bund, and Hechalutz. Isaac Zuckerman, for Hechalutz,
gave a report on the dreadful tidings from the provinces,
where Jews were still being put to death by mass extermination. The Warsaw Jews, he said, were unconvinced by
the illegal press that Lublin Jewry had been wiped out. It
was necessary, he felt, that the Warsaw Ghetto must defend
itself. To that end, he proposed the creation of a united
Jewish fighting force and a united front of all Jewish parties
to make contacts with the Polish underground and its
armed units, to build an organization on the "Aryan side"
for procuring weapons, and to set up secret arsenals in the

Ghetto. The resolution was supported by the Poale Zion and the Left Poale Zion, but not by the Bund, the most important organization represented. Its spokesman, Moritz Orzech, said, "It is too early to talk about united fronts. If fighting groups are necessary, each party should build its own. . . . You speak like children. Your words cannot be taken in earnest. All you want to do is create panic and undermine really useful work. As for a united Jewish party, the Bund is opposed to such a concept. The Bund has a Socialist, not a national Jewish, outlook. A completely Israelite organization is out of the question. We shall fight when the Poles are ready to fight—not now. We have our own strategy. We consider this whole meeting and your proposals nonsense." To save the face of the callers of the meeting, Orzech proposed to send out a propaganda statement, a document to give a psychological lift to the Ghetto. The others felt that to have such a statement as the sole result of the meeting would be farcical; they voted it down.

But neither the P.P.R. nor the young Zionists were to be put off. Another conference was held to which all proletarian and anti-Fascist groups were invited. The Bund sent no delegates, nor did the General Zionists. Those present (P.P.R., Poale Zion, Left Poale Zion, Dror, Hechalutz and Hashomer Hatzair) set up an Anti-Fascist Bloc. Its aims were the creation of anti-Fascist fighting units, formation of relief organizations for victims of the fight against Fascism, and unity of propaganda efforts in the struggle against reaction and passivity in the Ghetto. The executive committee of the Bloc consisted of Shachne Zagan (Left Poale Zion), Schmidt (P.P.R.), Joseph Sack (Poale Zion), Tsivia Lubetkin (Dror and Hechalutz), and

Mordecai Anielewicz (Hashomer Hatzair). Joseph Lewartowski took Schmidt's place after the latter's murder by
the Gestapo.

The fighting units were made up of groups of five.
Weaponless, they studied the theory of shooting, learned
the uses of dynamite and the making of mines, and prac-
ticed first-aid measures. Several hundred previously unaffiliated recruits soon joined the ranks of the activists.
Zukunft, the youth division of the Bund, against the orders
of the parent body, also joined. Propaganda took the form
of slogans: "Down with the Shops!" "Make grenades, not
watches!" To these dramatic but unfruitful slogans shortly
was added the publication, *Der Ruf* ("The Call"), the
organ of the Anti-Fascist Bloc. It was no more practical in
its advice than the slogans. It said, "The liberation of the
masses can come and will come with the victory of the Red
Army and of all those forces who wage war with it against
the common enemy. . . . The Jews of the Ghetto fight not
only in self-defense, not only for their honor, not only for
the overthrow of Fascism, but also for a free, new Poland.
. . . The Jews of the Ghetto must imitate the underground
movements of Europe. . . . Shoulder to shoulder, we must
unite against Hitler Fascism!"

The Germans took note of the pin-pricking propaganda.
During the early morning hours of April 18th, 52 Jews
were taken from their beds and shot on the streets in front
of their homes. The official reason for the lesson-teaching
executions was given out as "resistance to German authority." The Gestapo acted on a list compiled, it was said, by
informers. The victims were communal and cultural leaders, Bundists, Zionist youth leaders, underground workers

from several other groups, printers, and bakers. The last were chosen because they were the most important financial backers of the resistance movement. If the Nazis meant by this act of terror to frighten the Jews, to stop their subversive activities, they almost succeeded. The Anti-Facist Bloc was severely shaken.

Its cadres were further depleted in May by the departure from the Ghetto of a number of young workers for the Warsaw hinterland. In response to a call from the People's Guards, they volunteered to join up with the partisan bands already existing or being organized in those areas.

Another blow came on May 30th. On that day, just as they were carting a hand-press into the Ghetto, the P.P.R. leaders, Andrzej Schmidt and Samuel Zimmerman, together with David Wlasko, were captured, taken to the Pawiak prison, and shot.

The increased need for secrecy, the lack of general popular support, the indecisiveness as to tactics, all weakened the effectiveness of the Anti-Fascist Bloc in setting up a broad resistance movement. Nevertheless, acts of resistance still took place—to such an extent that, early in June, Auerswald, the German Commissioner, issued a warning that "terroristic acts and disobedience to police orders" would lead to immediate application of the principle of collective responsibility. As evidence of his sincerity, 110 Jews were taken from prison and shot, a bloody admonition to the Ghetto Jews.

No more was heard of the Anti-Fascist Bloc. It was superseded by another organization with similar aims, born during the devastating events of the next few months.

CHAPTER IV

July to September, 1942

ON July 21, 1942, the first mass liquidation of Warsaw Jewry started. The Germans announced that deportations would take place "for resettlement in the East." Their explanation seemed rational enough: Warsaw was to remain the center of Jewish production for German war needs; all nonproductive Jews would have to build a new life for themselves in a strictly segregated enclave in the conquered Soviet territories. The aid of Jewish authorities was enlisted to make the deportations as easy as possible—for the Germans. The *Judenrat* and the Jewish police co-operated completely, even to the extent of using the easing of the physical hunger of the people to induce them to appear voluntarily at the *Umschlagsplatz*, the deportation center.

Rumors and delusion spread through the Ghetto. Only 60,000 Jews were to be deported—only the troublemakers would go. The "new life in the East" would be freer. Now the Jews would be forced to do farm labor—not a bad idea in the eyes of some Jewish nationalists—now the Jews would be protected against anti-Semitic outbursts. Every story found its believers. The Germans helped to fortify the wishful thinking. Post cards came from "the East" describing the hard but full-bellied life in the new Jewish districts; inventories were made in factories and workshops so that the workers thought that their machines would soon be following them. Few realized that "resettlement" was another one of the many German euphemisms, this one for "death."

The political parties had to act quickly. An urgent meeting was called to which all organizations (except the Revisionists) were invited. The Bund met separately to consider its action, but sent delegates to the larger meeting to express its viewpoint. They took the position that resistance, in the absence of any arms, could only take the form of attempts by individuals to evade the deportation order and by the masses to fight the Jewish police at every step of the way. Any other type of resistance would doom the entire Ghetto, instead of no more than 60,000 Jews. Who would, convinced though he were that the Nazis meant the inevitable extermination of the whole Ghetto, dare take upon himself the responsibility for prematurely precipitating such a catastrophe?

Sixteen delegates were at the larger meeting. Present were: Eliezer Bloch, a cultural leader active in the Self-Help Agency and an adherent of a radical faction of the General Zionists; Samuel Breslau, from Hashomer Hatzair; Dr. Adolf Berman, from the Left Poale Zion; Isaac Zuckerman, from Hechalutz; Rabbi Zishe Friedman, from Agudah (Orthodox), and a member of the *Judenrat*; Joseph Lewartowski, from the P.P.R.; David Guzik and Isaac Giterman, from the Joint Distribution Committee;

Joseph Kaplan, from Hashomer Hatzair; Menachem Kirshenbaum, from the General Zionists; Alexander Landau, manager of a furniture factory and a fellow-traveler of the Left Poale Zion; Moritz Orzech, from the Bund; Dr. Emanuel Ringelblum, the keeper of the secret archives of Ghetto life and a member of the Left Poale Zion; Joseph Sack, from Poale Zion; Shachne Zagan, from the Left Poale Zion; and Dr. Ignatz Schipper, from Poale Zion. To the question "What is to be done?" only the Left Zionists, Hechalutz, and a few others spoke up for active resistance. Rabbi Friedman said, "I believe in God and a miracle. God will not permit his people to be destroyed. We must wait and a miracle will certainly take place. There is no sense in fighting the Germans. They can finish us off in a few days. . . . You, my friends, who turn to the Allies, do you or do you not believe that the Allies will eventually conquer and free you? You, my friends, who look to the Soviet revolutionary movement, do you or do you not believe in the final victory of the Red Army over capitalism? Dear friends, endure yet a while longer and freedom will come!" The majority, whose opinion was expressed by Dr. Schipper, wanted to wait until the situation was clarified, using as their arguments collective responsibility, just 60,000, no grounds for assuming that deportation meant anything as horrible as death, and so on. The Bund delegate said, "With my heart I'm with you, but cold logic holds me back."

The minority was dissatisfied with the decision. All the Left groups resolved to form a workers' committee for defense and resistance. On July 28th, a general staff of a Jewish Fighting Organization (*Zhydowska Organizacja*

Bojowa, hence acronymically *Zhob*) was constituted, made up of Tsivia Lubetkin, Mordecai Tenenbaum, Samuel Breslau, and Isaac Zuckerman. The total arsenal consisted of—one revolver. Fighters without weapons were a mockery, especially since hundreds of young men and women joined *Zhob* in their desire for vengeance. A delegation with "good visages" (Tosia Altman, Frumke Plotnitzki, Leah Perlstein, Arieh Willner) was sent to the "Aryan side" to make contact with the Polish underground to get arms. Meanwhile, *Zhob* put out handbills telling the masses that resettlement really meant death, that they should hide the women and children, that they should resist. Some, following the advice, fought barehanded and were killed on the spot. Most of the people they were trying to save greeted the distributors with blows and tore up the leaflets. The posters affixed to walls were defaced. *Zhob* members were denounced as *agents provocateurs.*

Something had to be done since no arms were forthcoming. *Zhob,* as well as the Bund and the P.P.R., made thousands of false documents and work cards for the unlucky, for those who were not able to show that they were "productive workers." Sentences of death were formally passed on Joseph Szerynski, the Jewish chief of police, and on other collaborators with the Germans; the actual executions had to wait until guns were available.

The P.P.R. issued its own leaflets, calling for struggle even without weapons, for attacking the Jewish police. Their slogan was: "Better an unequal fight than passivity!" They reasoned thus: The Jewish police would be forced to call on the Polish police for help; then the Germans would be forced to attack the Jews en masse; the attack would be the signal for a general uprising of the Polish population; and the initial sacrifice would serve to save the remainder of the Jews. In the interim, rescue missions should be undertaken and as many Jews as possible should be helped to escape to the "Aryan side," where Polish patriots were urged to give them help. A similar call to the Poles was put out by the Left Socialists of the "Socialist Poland" faction (outside the Ghetto).

Towards the end of July, the Bund had solid proof that the transports were not going to the East but to Treblinka, a camp for mass extermination in gas chambers. The news was brought by Zalman Friedrich from a railroad worker, who confirmed the earlier surmises that the Germans were lying. The Bund immediately put out a special edition of *Der Shturm,* in which they gave the horrible details of Treblinka and in which they raised the cry, "Do not go voluntarily." The *Judenrat* officials immediately denounced the story about Treblinka as a fabrication. And the Jewish masses, convinced of the truth, simultaneously clung to the logic-proof belief that only a part of the Jewish population was destined for destruction.

The Poles felt otherwise. The commanders of the London-directed underground forces, the *Armja Krajowa,* not at all friendly to the Jews and containing many out-and-out anti-Semites, met with General Stefan Rowecki to discuss what action they should take. Rowecki expounded his view that the Germans intended to kill all the Jews first, and then the Poles; therefore, for self-protection alone, the Poles should aid the Jews, thus frustrating the German plan. The other commanders opposed any direct help on the ground that if the United States and Great Britain, with all their rich resources and air forces, were unable to stop the Nazi crimes in the other occupied countries, how could the weak Polish underground hope to do any better in Poland? Furthermore, it was reported that those Jewish leaders in touch with the *Armja Krajowa* were sanguine about the future; they did not expect more than 60,000 Jews to be killed. The Jews' formal request for arms was passed over. Their other request was granted—to forward an appeal to the Polish government-in-exile in London to put pressure on the Allies to threaten reprisals against German nationals in the Allied countries unless the deportations were stopped. The appeal was ignored in London, probably through the influence of those Polish reactionaries who publicly and cynically said, "The Germans are decisively ending the Jewish question in Poland."

General Sikorsky, the commander-in-chief of the military forces under the direction of the émigré government, tried to overcome this overt anti-Semitism by pointing out that the British and Americans had made democracy the slogan of their war effort and that anti-Semitism was condemned by all circles in the West, even by conservatives and Catholics. His efforts to convince his colleagues bore as little fruit in Poland as in London.

Other underground forces were more willing to help the Jews. The P.P.R. arranged for Tosia Altman to bring into the Ghetto five revolvers and eight grenades from the "Aryan side"; she was caught, and the weapons confiscated, but she herself managed to escape. The People's Guards aided young workers in leaving the Ghetto to join the partisans in the forests. A group of about thirty from Dror and Hashomer Hatzair made their way with difficulty to the

woods only to find themselves in a situation almost as peri-
lous as in the Ghetto. They were still unarmed and were
defenseless against attacks from the German soldiers and
anti-Semitic bands of the *Armja Krajowa*. Many were
killed before a remnant succeeded in returning to the
Ghetto. Out of others who left the Ghetto in the hope that
their fight against the Nazis would be more effective as
guerrillas only a few were not disappointed. Trade with the
organized partisans was more successful. In exchange for
sending doctors to them and for German uniforms stolen
from the factories, the People's Guards bartered war material. So, on one occasion, Arieh Willner brought in fifty
grenades and some explosive materials.

The increasing tempo and brutality of the deportations spread a black pall of despair throughout the Ghetto.
The workers' resistance movement, none too strong to start
with, grew weaker day by day. Merely maintaining contact
was a tremendous task. Communications were cut off.
Crossing the street was like walking in No-Man's-Land
between front lines. Even going from house to house was
dangerous. The Bund, getting sympathy but no weapons
from its Socialist contacts on the "Aryan side," disbanded
its fighting groups. The P.P.R.—its leader, Lewartowski,
arrested and killed, and its cells broken up—tried to lift
flagging spirits by calling for a Second Front. The young
Zionists became disheartened, especially after their leadership was depleted by the loss, among others, of Joseph
Kaplan and Samuel Breslau. And yet the resistance limped
along.

On August 20th, Israel Kanal, disguised as a policeman,
made the long-awaited attempt on the life of Szerynski but

succeeded only in wounding, not killing, him. Over a hundred fires were set in various factories producing war materials and in warehouses where goods taken from the deported Jews were kept. Fired to enthusiasm by each minor achievement, the resistance movement was cast into the depths by each misadventure. The Selections Office at 103 Zelazna was mined, but the electrical connections were poor and no explosion resulted. A pitifully small arsenal, painfully gathered together, was found and taken by the Germans.

Less fruitless was the propaganda. The Jews finally were convinced about the awful news of Treblinka and began to hide, for help came not from the mountains or the Allies or world Jewry. Indeed, aid from the Jews in the Allied countries was forbidden by the Allied powers on the technical ground that the Ghetto Jews were still citizens of an occupied country and to help them would be to help the Nazis. Only the bombardment of Warsaw during the night of August 21st by Soviet planes gave the Jews the feeling that their peril was not unknown to the world; they interpreted the attack as an attempt to stop the German murderers from completing their job of extermination.

Nothing stopped the Germans. The "resettlement" went on until September 30th. When the "action" was finally over, out of 350,000 Jews at the beginning of July, between 50,000 and 70,000 remained (the figures vary, depending on the source of information). The surviving Jews were herded together in four areas of the former Ghetto (see map).

CHAPTER V

September, 1942, to January, 1943

THE Central Ghetto (A on the map) was the largest division. It contained, besides the fateful *Umschlagsplatz*, the offices of the *Judenrat* and its institutions, and the houses assigned to them as living quarters for their personnel. It also held the *Werterfassung*, the S.S. organization responsible for the reception and disposition of Jewish goods. All the inhabitants were counted as "nonproductive Jews," except for the workers (and their families) living in six houses on Nalewki Street, attached to Brauer's, the only factory in the district.

The Productive Ghetto (B) was worthy of its name. It contained the factories and warehouses of the German industrialists Toebbens, Schultz (the "big shop"), K. G. Schultz (the "little shop"), Rehrich, Hoffman, and Hallman and Schilling. Each factory had houses assigned to it for its workers, as well as its own commissary, and often a prison.

The Small Ghetto(C) held another Toebbens factory and the workers' quarters allotted to it.

The smallest of the Ghettos was the Brushmakers' (D).

In this one large block were concentrated the factories that made all kinds of brushes for the German Army (from toothbrushes to heavy floor brushes). In the same area were the factory workers' dwellings.

Between the Central and the Productive Ghettos was a "neutral" zone. No one was allowed to live there; death was the penalty for trespassing. The section between the Productive and the Small Ghettos was to become part of "Aryan" Warsaw once all the buildings had been searched and cleared of everything the Jews had left behind. In actuality, the deserted areas were inhabited—by "wild" Jews, "illegals" who had not received "right-to-live" cards, work certificates or "numbers" stating they were necessary for the functioning of the community. They hid in cellars, attics, and closets, and lived, if it could be called living, until they were caught and killed by the Gestapo. Polish thieves, too, had their hideouts there, as well as the smugglers who thrived on bringing in food and taking out people for hard cash, American dollars, jewelry, and other valuables.

The Germans promulgated new rules. No one was permitted to be on the street without special permission. Movement from one factory to another was not allowed. Workers were marched in groups from their houses to the factories. Even the sick on the way to the hospital had to be escorted by police. Violation of the orders was punished by immediate shooting on the spot or by arrest for transportation to Treblinka. Work in the factories was controlled by the special factory police units especially set up for that purpose.

Under such conditions it might have been expected that

the resistance would have given up in despair. Not so. When the deportations stopped, the Jews had a breathing spell, a time in which soul-searching evaluations took place. The terror they had gone through, the gaping empty streets, the loss of their loved ones—all brought to the fore the sharp question of why the Ghetto had not fought back. Dr. Ringelblum, the historian, said bitterly, "The 'resettlement' should not have been permitted. We should have run out into the streets, set fire to everything in sight, torn down the walls, escaped to the Other Side. The Germans would have taken their revenge. It would have cost tens of thousands of lives, but not 300,000. Now we are ashamed of ourselves, disgraced in our own eyes and in the eyes of the world, where our docility earned us nothing. This must not be repeated now. We must put up a resistance, defend ourselves against the enemy, man and child." His attitude was not unique. All illusions about the Germans had gone by the board. The Jews realized that those still alive were alive by chance, were living on sufferance, that the next liquidation would be the last.

The conservative elements in the Bund were forced to give way to the "hotheads," the young men and women who had preached resistance to their elders' deaf ears, crying out in vain for a united front of all Jews against the Germans. Now they began to push an active campaign for unity, for an armed, really armed, resistance, for revenge and honor. The P.P.R. pulled itself together and reassembled its cadres, reorganizing its fighting groups under the command of Michael Rosenfeld, a close friend of Mordecai Anielewicz. A Jewish National Committee consisting of Poale Zion, Left Poale Zion, Hechalutz, Dror,

Hashomer Hatzair, Gordonia, Hitachdut, and General Zionists was formed; later, all the other parties joined the Committee with the exception of the Revisionists and the Bund. The leaders of both Poale Zion factions finally won over the Bund leadership, which was also influenced by the steady loss of its young people to other groups. To save face or to preserve its integrity as a non-nationalist Jewish party, the Bund did not actually become part of the Jewish National Committee but instead co-operated with a co-ordinating committee, the military arm of which was a new *Zhob* (Jewish Fighting Organization). On October 20, 1942, the organizational form of the latter was decided upon.

The Presidium was made up of Isaac Zuckerman (Hashomer Hatzair), Menachem Kirshbaum (General Zionists), and Abraham Blum (Bund). The other members of the Plenum were Ephraim Fondaminski (P.P.R.), Miriam Heinsdorf (Hashomer Hatzair), Melech Feinkind (Left Poale Zion), Eliezer Geller (Gordonia), Tsivia Lubetkin (Hechalutz and Dror), and Jochanan Morgenstern (Poale Zion).

Commander-in-Chief of *Zhob* was Mordecai Anieliewicz, 23 years old, a young man of great personal charm, highly regarded by all the parties. Isaac Zuckerman was Vice-Commander, in charge of weapons procurement. Other staff members were Marek Edelman (Bund), in charge of intelligence; Morgenstern, in charge of finances; and Rosenfeld and Hersh Berlinski (Left Poale Zion), in charge of operations. Subcommittees were made up of: propaganda—Blum, Zuckerman, and Feinkind; finances —Heinsdorf, Lubetkin, and Morgenstern; supplies—Tuvia

Borzykowski (Hechalutz) and Judah Wengrower (Hash-omer Hatzair).

A civilian commission was organized for procurement, for the building of bunkers (dugouts used as hiding places), and for the spreading of propaganda about active resistance. It consisted of Eliezer Bloch (General Zionists), David Cholodenko (Bund), Isaac Giterman and David Guzik (Joint Distribution Committee), Menachem Kohn, Alexander Landau, and Joseph Sack (Left Poale Zion). To work on the "Aryan side" with the Polish underground governing committee Dr. Adolf Berman was assigned as representative of the Jewish National Committee, and Arieh Willner as representative of *Zhob*.

A new spirit entered into the entire resistance movement. Gone were the suspicions, the doctrinal arguments, the memories of past quarrels, the dreams of Paradise and Zion and the Brotherhood of Man. All were united in one immediate task—to build up *Zhob* to become an effective fighting force against the Germans.

First, the morale of the masses had to be revived. And the first step in doing that was to demonstrate that *Zhob* meant what it said when it proscribed informers and collaborators. On October 29th, Jacob Leikin, the commander of the Jewish police, successor to Szerynski, was assassinated by Elihu Rozhanski near the police office at 4 Gensia Street. Communiqués from *Zhob* were posted in the Ghetto, stating that the execution was carried out on its order after judgment had been passed, and that sentences had also been pronounced on "the presidium of the Warsaw *Judenrat* for collaboration with the occupying forces and for signing death warrants, on factory directors and administrators who abuse and oppress their workers, and on the leaders and officers of the factory police for their bestial wickedness toward the 'illegal' Jewish population. Rigorous action will be taken to carry out the judgments."

Exactly one month later, Israel First, the head of the economic section of the *Judenrat,* a go-between for the Nazis, was assassinated by David Shulman.

Morale-building included the issuance of publications to assure the remaining Jews in the Ghetto that a resistance movement still existed and that it had a positive program. Leaflets and one-page news bulletins came out in Yiddish and Polish, the most widely circulated being *Wiadomosci* ("Information"). The Jews were warned against German perfidy, against the new rumors of a stabilized Ghetto, against registrations and controls. They were told to hide, to make secret places for concealment during the time of renewed terror that was sure to come, to fight with sticks and stones, if necessary. They were advised to smash the machines and burn the factories when orders came for evacuation. The call on December 4 ended with the stirring words, "Remember that you—the civilian Jewish population—are also on the front lines in the battle for freedom and humanity! . . . Long live liberty!"

The Jews did not need to have the slogans repeated very often. Under guise of building air-raid shelters, they constructed bunkers, underground (literally and figuratively) hide-outs. The bunkers varied in size and safety. Some were small, with only one entrance. Others were very large, with several rooms and escape exits, sometimes to sewers and sometimes through tunnels to "neutral" houses. Some were electrified, some were candlelit; some had food-storage bins, some were bare-walled. One thing they all had in common—the entrances were well hidden, known only to the builders, behind closet doors, double walls, stairways, ovens.

Zhob was not content with propaganda activities. It foresaw that leaving the Jews in the Ghetto meant their sure death. It therefore made arrangements with friendly Poles on the "Aryan side" for hiding places and for false documents and identification cards for escaped Jews. At first, only the P.P.R. and the Left Socialists cooperated in this work; later a Polish Council for Aid to Jews was organized, the Bund delegate to which was Dr. Leon Feiner. The Council was made up of patriots, humanitarians, nonpolitical and political figures from the intelligentsia and the working class; official delegates were assigned from the Right and Left Socialist parties, the Peasants' Party, the two branches of the Democratic Party, the Jewish National Committee, and the Bund. It was an official subcommittee of the underground government; its duties were to supply Jews with false papers and safe living quarters, to help place Jewish children in orphan asylums and convents and with foster parents, to raise money for arms for the Jews. The Council, known acronymically as *Zhegota*, was credited with saving at least 20,000 Jews up to the time of the final destruction of the Ghetto.

Advice and evasive tactics were not what *Zhob* meant by resistance. Resistance, to leaders and followers alike, meant fighting. The procurement of weapons meant the difference between empty mouthings and armed combat. *Zhob* made very effort to get arms and ammunition. Each political division tried to outdo the others in obtaining arms. Requests were made of the *Armja Krajowa,* known to have large hidden stores of weapons. At a secret meeting on November 11th, General Rowecki and his staff praised *Zhob* for its activity in mobilizing the Jewish people, but it was not until the end of December that ten old revolvers of small calibre, in poor condition, with a few rounds of ammunition, were delivered to the Ghetto; and that took place only through the firm intercession of one member of the London government. General Rowecki expressed his fears that such arms would be used by the Communists for their own ends, and said he would give no more. Negotiations with General Rola-Zymierski of the People's Guards were more, but not much more, fruitful. The People's Guards themselves were poorly armed at that time; nevertheless, thirteen revolvers and seventeen grenades were sent in, and a few rifles later in December.

The Jewish National Committee sent an appeal to New York, addressed to Rabbi Stephen Wise, Dr. Goldmann, the Workmen's Circle, and the Joint Distribution Committee, asking for immediate retaliatory acts against the Germans, for arrangements to save the children, and for money to buy weapons for "our lives and honor." It ended with the heart-rending cry, "Brothers! The remnant of the Jews in Poland lives in the ever-present knowledge that in the most fearful days of our history you have given us no help! Arouse yourselves! This is our last appeal to you!"

Zhob realized that it would have to get its arms by itself. The Bundist, Michael Klepfisch, made contact with a Pole, Stefan Macho, a former co-worker in a metal factory. The latter's flat became the center for other contacts and for the temporary storage of arms bought for the most part in the black market on Kazimierz Square from Poles who worked in arms factories or from others who stole weapons from army dumps they were supposed to be guarding. The P.P.R. had a group led by the worker Kosowski and the ex-smuggler and athlete Samuel Koenigstein; they made contacts with individuals from the People's Guards, through Eugenia Piwinski; their meeting place was Parisowski Square. Thieves and smugglers in the "neutral" zone were recruited into the search for arms; they entered willingly because the Jews paid high prices and the business was profitable. Even two German soldiers, known only as Walter and Max, gave arms for the "anti-fascist cause." The supply of arms was only a trickle, withal. Most of the weapons had to be manufactured in the Ghetto by the Jews themselves. Besides making "Molotov cocktails," flasks filled with incendiary and explosive materials, the Ghetto workers repaired old and broken-down guns. Under the leadership of Isaac Suknik, a former sergeant in the Polish militia and an expert metal worker, two workshops for the manufacture of small arms were organized; his assistants in this work were the Fondaminskis (Ephraim and Liba, his wife), Moishe Yagojinski, and Michael Klepfisch.

Arms were slowly accumulated with pain and woe, and then were insufficient. By the end of December, 1942, only two groups of Dror and Hechalutz were fully armed and ready; the others were symbolically given one or two grenades or guns.

Recruitment of fighters was not difficult but had to be done with great care because of the danger from informers. Some volunteers were taken into the *Zhob* groups imme-

diately, others only after a probationary period. Training
was given in military tactics, but more important was the
inculcation of selfless idealism. *Zhob* became a school for
character-building as well as for warfare.

One party did not seek weapons. That was Agudah, the
party of the Orthodox Jews. There were practically no religious youths left in the Ghetto after the July deportations,
for obvious reasons. Those Jews that had been spared were
the "productive elements," workers and strong young men
inured to hard labor by their previous occupations or by
their participation in the physical culture and sports groups
of the pre-war Zionist movement. The traditionally dressed
Talmudic students, pale and soft-handed, quietists and
Hasidim, were among the first victims of the Nazis.

Two Ghetto groups, besides *Zhob*, one organized and
one unorganized, were armed. The Revisionists, whose
fighting branch was the Jewish Military Union, led by Dr.
David Wdowinski, maintained headquarters at 7-9 Muranowska Street, where they had an arms magazine. Its Political Committee was headed by Leib Rodal and Dr. Michael
Strykowski; the technical-military commander was Paul
Frenkel. The fighters lived communally, away from their
families, for security reasons. Two sections were hidden in
the Productive Ghetto and one in the Brushmakers'. The
main section was divided into six units, located at 1, 3, 5,
7-9, and 40 Muranowska Street; each unit had a nucleus of
twenty *Betarim* (members of a Revisionist circle) with
other non-party but vengeful young Jews. The Jewish Military Union had established relations with some branches of
the Polish underground movement; the latter provided
them with instructors for training in the use of arms, in

street fighting, in barricade warfare, and in defense of the bunkers. More important, they received weapons and ammunition, machine guns and hand grenades. Their contact with the Polish military was through Captain Caesar Ketling, a leader in the secret Democratic Party. By the end of December, 1943, the Jewish Military Union had 400 trained members.

The unorganized "wild" groups were a mixture of idealists and individualists bent on vengeance, unwilling to submit to military discipline, and of gangsters and opportunists. Some of the latter used their weapons to rob their fellow Jews of money so that they could buy false papers or bribe the wall guards and escape from the Ghetto. Several bands specialized in posing as *Zhob* supporters and, as such, made levies on individuals "to buy arms." Others adopted "American" methods of kidnaping and ransom. Others were undisguised thieves. *Zhob* had to wage a relentless struggle against the "wild" groups. Some of the "wild ones" were finally convinced that they could fight the Germans best by joining *Zhob*; others were killed by the Germans or the wall guards and occasionally by *Zhob* adherents; others simply disappeared.

Zhob, despite the shortage of arms, began to feel its mettle. It made two tryouts of its strength; it overcame the German guards in the prison at Schultz's factory on Nowolipie Street and freed over 100 "illegal" Jews being held there for transport to Treblinka. In the same area in broad daylight it held up the factory bakery and took from it the entire day's supply of bread.

The time seemed ready for action. The date was tentatively set for January 22, 1943.

CHAPTER VI

The January Uprising: January, 18-20, 1943

SABOTAGE and attacks on Germans by Poles had been increasing during the last months of 1942 and the beginning of January, 1943. Partisan activity in the Warsaw countryside was on the increase. No great damage was done but there was enough to annoy the Germans. Berlin took note. Himmler ordered on January 11th that immediate steps be taken to put down the unrest, to confine those "proletarian elements" linked with the "bandits" (as the Germans called the partisans) and send them to concentration camps. The order was issued after his personal heavily guarded inspection tour of the Warsaw district, in which he did not neglect the "Jewish Residential District."

Himmler expressed his anger at finding the Ghetto still so large despite his definite instructions of October 10, 1942, that all the Jews were to be removed from Warsaw. In a secret letter to Obergruppenführer Frederick-Wilhelm Krueger, in charge of S.S. police operations, he ordered the military and police authorities to carry out his orders without fail, the action to be completed by February 15, 1943. He said that he was surprised that 40,000 (German figure)

Jews were still in the Ghetto, that a maximum of 16,000
was all that was needed for the slave-labor camps, that the
others, starting with an immediate 8,000, were to be "resettled," that no excuses would be taken. German industrialists, especially Toebbens, he charged, were waxing fat on
their war profits; they could learn patriotism better, he
hinted, on the Eastern Front. He ordered the machines and
raw materials to be removed at once to the S.S. labor
camps in the Lublin district. Obergruppenführer Ferdinand
von Sammern-Frankenegg and Chief of Security Police Dr.
Hahn were given full responsibility to see that his decree
was obeyed.

Of course, *Zhob* knew nothing of Himmler's orders. It
chose January 22nd as the day for an armed attack on the
Nazis because that day would be the six-month anniversary
of the beginning of the great July deportations. Leaflets
were surreptitiously distributed in all the four Ghetto areas,
telling the Jews to be ready, to be on the watch, to attack
when attacked, to die fighting rather than with folded
hands. The actual date of the uprising was known to only a
few, such was the fear of Gestapo informers.

The armed demonstration never came off. On Monday,
January 18th, von Sammern-Frankenegg started the so-
stringently-commanded deportations. He expected no trouble. As a matter of fact, he had invited a guest to be present
at the "action," S.S. Hauptsturmführer Theodor von
Eupen-Malmedy, the commander of the Treblinka camp.
The factory directors were told to have their workers report
at the *Umschlagsplatz* for "selections." Heavy detachments
of military and police units were stationed around the walls.

Zhob was taken by surprise. Its forces were scattered, its arsenals inaccessible. It put out a hastily mimeographed leaflet in Polish, saying:

Jews!
The enemy has moved on to the second phase of your extermination!
Do not resign yourselves to death! Defend yourselves!
Grab an axe, an iron bar, a knife!
Let them take you this way, if they can!
Remember, in battle lies your only hope of being saved!
Fight!

The advice was unnecessary. Some workers, indeed, went voluntarily, but by far the greater majority hid in cellars, attics, secret rooms, and previously prepared bunkers.

Fighting broke out immediately. At 30 Gensia Street, Emily Landau, a 17-year-old member of the Hashomer Hatzair, threw a grenade at the troops. Several were wounded but she herself was killed in the counterattack.

At the corner of Zamenhof and Mila Streets, Mordecai Anielewicz led his group, armed with five revolvers, five grenades, Molotov cocktails, iron bars, and stones, in an attack on a German detail escorting a throng of Jews to the *Umschlagsplatz*. The attack succeeded in making the Germans withdraw long enough to allow the captured Jews to scatter and escape. Reinforced, the Germans returned and mowed down most of the fighters. Anielewicz was caught but managed to escape. The few left alive withdrew to barricade themselves in a house on Niska Street, where they tried to keep the Germans from entering by setting fire to the stairs. All were eventually killed.

In another house on Niska Street, the porter, Samuel Champel, led a group in an unequal conflict; all the Jews fell in the battle.

The fighting groups quickly realized that street fighting was too costly for them, unprepared and short of weapons as they were. They switched to what they called "partisan tactics." They hid in houses and fired on the Germans from cover, then fled when the Germans entered the houses; they allowed German patrols to enter courtyards and then attacked from every side. Such actions took place at 40 Zamenhof Street, 44 Muranowska Street, 34 Mila Street and 22 Franciskańska Street. The Germans suffered casualties, but the Jews suffered more because of the lack of weapons. Some groups were more successful. That led by Zechariah Artstein (of Dror), for example, with only four revolvers and four grenades, lost one man in driving out a German patrol but killed two Germans and were able to despoil them of their weapons and ammunition. Most of the fighting occurred in the Central Ghetto because there the *Zhob* groups were made up of young Zionists living communally, thus needing no call to come together for action.

In the Productive Ghetto fighting took place on a smaller but no less courageous scale, considering that weapons were even scarcer than in the Central Ghetto. There were four groups, led by Benjamin Leibgut, Bronek Jaworski, Israel Kanal, and David Nowogrodski; amongst all four there were but four pistols and one grenade. Their plan was to throw the grenade into a squad of soldiers and then set fire to the Schultz factory in the ensuing confusion. The grenade did not go off. They hastily withdrew to 78

Leszno Street, where, incredibly, using boiling water, acid, sticks and stones, they drove off the Germans, but not without losing Benjamin Leibgut and Abraham Feiner in the fray.

Near the *Umschlagsplatz* a group of fighters infiltrated a column of workers being led to deportation; at a given signal, grenades were thrown at the guards. In the confused hand-to-hand combat that followed, weapons were taken away from the guards and most of the workers fled to safety.

At the *Umschlagsplatz*, 60 Jews refused to go into the freight cars and fought the Germans barehanded. All were killed.

The Brushmakers' groups had no weapons at all. It was from this section that most of the impressed workers were taken away.

Sporadic fighting continued until January 20th, when von Sammern-Frankenegg ordered the withdrawal of the troops from the Ghetto. To continue the action in the same way would now be useless, he thought. The Jews were too well hidden; now that they knew the Jews had weapons, the Germans feared to make any intensive searches in cellars and houses. Altogether, 6500 Jews had been removed from the Ghetto. The quota ordered by Himmler could not be reached because of the unexpected Jewish resistance. Twenty Germans and two Polish auxiliaries had been killed and 50 more wounded—a number trivial enough except for its psychological effect.

That effect it undoubtedly had. Samuel Winter, a well-known intellectual, kept up his diary while he was hidden in a bunker during the fighting. He notes:

I heard rumors that Jews were fighting in Niska and
Zamenhof Streets—members of Hashomer and *Halutzim*
[Pioneers]. What kind of ideas do they have—these idealists? What will be the consequences? I rather think that
from a historical point of view and also with regard to the
future the work of the Historical Commission *Oneg Shabbat*
is more important than the fighting of the Jews. . . . Today
3,000 Jews were taken. . . .

But the next day he says,

. . . the Germans are afraid to enter the cellars and bunkers. . . .

And the next:

. . . the Germans withdrew and left the Ghetto. I think that
the fighting of the young men has forced them to do this. . . .

That Jews fought and that their resistance, feeble as it
was, was enough to make the Germans interrupt the deportations buoyed up the spirits of the Jews, now more than
ever aware of their desperate situation.

Zhob took immediate advantage of the new turn of
mind. Despite the fact that of the 50 groups it had before
January 18th only five were left, *Zhob* became next to the
Germans the most important power in the Ghetto.

CHAPTER VII

January to April, 1943

THE unexpectedness of the German move on January 18th had a double effect on *Zhob*. It was forced to recognize its weaknesses: insufficiency of weapons, absence of a previously prepared plan of co-ordinated action between the various groups, inadequacy of liaison between them, lack of guards to warn of surprises. It also took note of its strengths: its success in stopping the deportations, its influence over the Ghetto masses, its unforeseen power of daunting the Germans. *Zhob* took immediate steps to overcome its weaknesses and take advantage of its strengths.

The first thing it had to do was to regroup its scattered and shattered forces. New recruits and old veterans were joined in 22 fighting units, each made up for the most part but—an important point—not entirely of people with similar ideologies. The command was divided, with a commander in charge of each of the Ghettos and a supreme command under the direction of Mordecai Anielewicz. Each group adopted the communal style of living previously used only by the Revisionists and the young Zionists; thus any further surprise attack by the Germans would find them together, ready to fight.

Communal living had other advantages. Each group had
its own bunker and, later, its own arsenal. Each group was
now able to study and discuss tactics and techniques to be
used in the coming uprising. Most important, each group
fostered a feeling of kinship in its members. Already united
in their desire for vengeance on the Germans, they became
further attached by the psychic understanding that came
from close physical contact. Changes were made in personnel on the basis of qualifications, not on party lines.
Bundists and Communists were commanded by Zionists,
and Zionists by Bundists and Communists. Old polemics
about the future were forgotten in fraternal discussions
about the best way to insure the success of the coming
uprising. Such unity, however, did not interfere with each
political faction's remaining in touch with its associates
elsewhere. The Bund relied on help from the Polish Socialists and the *Armja Krajowa*; the Communists, from the
P.P.R. and the People's Guards; the Zionists, from the Jews
abroad. But all agreed that the help forthcoming, if any,
would be taken as support for *Zhob* and not for any individual constituent thereof.

The *Zhob* command co-ordinated the activities of the
fighting units and their sympathizers. By means of a con-
stant stream of verbal and printed propaganda, it called on
the Jews of the Ghetto to save themselves by evasion if
outright resistance was impossible. *Zhob* had to provide
hiding places for its members, collect arms and ammunition, train the enthusiastic raw recruits, establish security
measures, and make itself the mainspring of life in the
Ghetto. With the new spirit derived from the January actions, encouraged also by the visible expressions of support

from both the Left and the Right Polish underground
forces, it took up its tasks with a will.

The safety of the civilian population in the Ghetto had to
be insured. *Zhob* understood only too well that no resistance there could be wholly successful, that the Germans
would never tolerate an island of armed Jews in the midst
of occupied Warsaw. The Jews in the Ghetto had to be
saved; otherwise resistance would be glorious, heroic, but
only a romantic gesture, an act of desperation. The Jews
had to be kept out of the hands of the Nazis and then
removed from the walled Ghetto. The latter, *Zhob* felt,
could be done during the excitement and disturbance of an
armed uprising, when the walls would be breached and the
Jews could escape to be lost in "Aryan" Warsaw and its sub-
urbs or in the forests with the partisans. The task was difficult but not impossible. The experience of January had
taught *Zhob* that.

With *Zhob's* encouragement, a wave of building over-
took the Ghetto. The pre-existing bunkers were remodeled
and enlarged; new ones were constructed. Engineers and
architects were impressed for this work. With primitive
techniques and limited material, under the very noses of
the Nazis a veritable underground labyrinth came into
being. *Zhob* built its bunkers to serve as bases for its partisan warfare, as a hinterland for retreat when necessary.
The masses built theirs for safety. Ingenuity abounded.
Under the cellars of houses, sub-cellars were dug, leading
into an expanded cavern at the other end. In other cellars
the floor was removed, a sub-basement built, then the floor
replaced. Entrances were carefully concealed. Exits were
made multiple so that escape would be possible. Com-

municating tunnels led to other bunkers, to the outside through courtyards, to the sewer system, even to selected areas on the "Aryan" side. Thus the Jewish side of Muranowska Street was joined to the "Aryan" side, 74 Leszno Street to an "Aryan" house two blocks away, the Ghetto part of Karmelitzka Street to the Polish part. A network of tunnels led from the bunkers to the Catholic and Jewish cemeteries outside the Ghetto walls. Some tunnels led to houses in the "neutral zone," or to the "wild streets," and from there other tunnels linked the four divisions of the Ghetto. Most of the bunkers were connected with a water source. Many had electrical connections; others were candlelit. The great problem was ventilation because of the limited number of air vents.

Connections were also established over roof-tops and through passageways knocked through attics to join one row of houses to another. As a matter of fact, walking in the streets became so dangerous for the Jews that they took to going through the attics as a matter of course. With sardonic humor, one particularly busy attic thoroughfare was nicknamed the "Jewish Autostrada."

The main headquarters bunker of *Zhob* was located at 18 Mila Street. At 29, another bunker with a radio served as a central ammunition depot. Other *Zhob* bunkers were at 9 Mila, 22 Franciskańska, 33, 35, 37 Nalewki, 39 Świentojerska, 56 and 74 Leszno, and 69 Nowolipie Streets.

Simultaneously with the building of the bunkers, *Zhob* carried on an intensive campaign to get weapons. All the old contacts were utilized and new ones sought out with less difficulty than previously. The January events had made a great impression on the Poles. Patriotic Poles realized that by helping the Jews they were helping to defeat the German occupiers and they took more part in trying to arm the Jews. The *Armja Krajowa* sent in, at the end of February, 50 revolvers, 50 hand grenades, and four kilograms of explosives. The People's Guards sent in a few rifles and ammunition, but, as before January, by far the greatest supply of arms was brought into the Ghetto by the Jews themselves, arms bought from smugglers and underworld characters on the "Aryan side" eager for fast and huge profits.

The methods used for bringing in material were varied. Pfeiffer's leather factory on Okopowa Street bordered on the Ghetto. At night the watchman's eyes and ears were closed by a fat bribe, and boxes of ammunition were brought into the factory and pushed through a window on the other side into the Ghetto. Messengers met agents in the deserted "wild" houses and exchanged cash for dynamite that had to be secreted in their clothing, an ever-present source of danger as they crawled through the roof passages or the tunnels. Guns, hidden under kindling wood, were carted in wheelbarrows across Warsaw and then thrown over the walls. Two thousand litres of gasoline were bought and taken into the Ghetto in small quantities at a time.

Getting arms and ammunition was often accompanied by disappointment and frustration, dependent, as *Zhob's* emissaries were, on sharpers. In one case 6000 zlotys were paid out for four boxes of dynamite and three revolvers and only three boxes of dynamite were delivered. In another, a number of revolvers and hand grenades were sold to Arieh Willner on the "Aryan side"; shortly after he had

hidden them in his room there, the Gestapo came and arrested him and took away the little arsenal; he had been
informed on by the seller. Sometimes Poles on the lookout
near the Ghetto walls for escaping Jews they could black-
mail held up the messengers and took the money that was
to pay for weapons.

The urgency of the situation made the Jews willing to
pay any price for weapons. As a result of the great demand
and the short supply, prices rose rapidly. Vis (Polish-
made) or Parabellum (German-made) guns cost 12,000
zlotys each; one bullet cost 80 to 100 zlotys; grenades sold
for 10,000 to 15,000 zlotys apiece. The gasoline, acid, and
potassium needed to make explosives became equally ex-
pensive.

All over the Ghetto the hidden workshops for making
Molotov cocktails, bombs, and grenades speeded up their
activities. Yet, no matter how hard they worked, nor to
what extent they disregarded the dangers of smuggling, the
members of *Zhob* remained poorly armed. A letter from
Anielewicz to the Warsaw representative of the Polish government-in-exile dated March 18 states:

> The situation becomes daily more critical. Fifteen hun-
> dred men from the Schultz workshop must leave today. We
> expect "actions" in the Ghetto and workshops. The affair of
> the Brushmakers [who refused to leave voluntarily] that
> ended with our complete victory showed the enemy once and
> for all the resistance he could expect against his brutal and
> violent methods. In the next few days the end may come for
> Warsaw Jewry.
>
> Are we prepared? Materially, very poorly. Out of 49 guns
> [sent by the *Armja Krajowa*], only 39 are usable because of

the lack of ammunition for the others. Our arms situation worsens continually as a result of our activities in recent weeks, in which we used much ammunition. Now we have only ten rounds per weapon. This is catastrophic.

I request that you inform the authorities in our name that, unless arms reach us in quantity without delay, we shall regard the authorities as indifferent to the fate of Warsaw Jewry.

Giving weapons without ammunition creates an impression of cynical mockery about our fate and upholds the assumption that anti-Semitic feeling continues to be active among those in authority in Poland despite the cruel and tragic experiences of the last three years.

We do not have to convince anyone of our fighting ability and readiness to take up arms. Since January 18th the Jewish community in Warsaw has been in a state of continuous warfare with the invader and his servants. Whoever denies or doubts this is a vicious anti-Semite.

We expected that the authorities and their representatives would not only show "understanding" of our cause, but would look on the murder of millions of Jews, Polish citizens, as a prime problem of the day.

Unfortunately, we have no way of directly getting in touch with the Allied governments, the Polish government-in-exile, or Jewish organizations abroad to inform them about our situation and the treatment given us by the collaborating Polish authorities and public.

Dear Sirs! I ask you to take appropriate measures immediately with the military and governmental authorities. I ask that you read them this letter and demand persistently that they supply us with at least 100 hand grenades, 50 revolvers, ten rifles, and several thousand rounds of ammunition of various calibres.

I am ready to provide you within two days with the plans
of our positions, with maps, which should dispel any doubts
as to the necessity of supplying us with arms.

(signed) MALACHI [pseudonym of Anielewicz]
P.S.: The situation is tense. A group of our fighters this
morning attacked two members of the German Factory Police who for days have been terrorizing the Jewish population by shooting and robbery. One was killed at once, the
other while escaping. S.A. men and police interfered; one
S.A. man was badly wounded. We had no casualties. The
streets were deserted. We anxiously await developments.

By April, *Zhob* calculated that each fighter had one gun
with ten to fifteen rounds of ammunition, four or five hand
grenades, and a like number of Molotov cocktails. There
were two or three rifles in each group and one machine gun
for the entire Jewish Fighting Organization force.

Hard as it was to come by weapons, it was almost as
difficult to pay for them. Despite the fact that the resistance
fighters lived on black bread and marmalade, they could
not from their own resources get enough money together to
pay for their military needs. Taxation and "expropriation"
went hand in hand with arms-procurement and bunker-
building. The *Judenrat* itself was forced to contribute to the
fighting fund: it paid over 250,000 zlotys in three days, and
another 710,000 zlotys were paid from its economic section. Wealthy Jews were arbitrarily taxed. Some, like the
revered Abraham Gepner, co-operated completely; others
objected, bargained, then paid; others refused outright.
These last were arrested by *Zhob* and held until their families ransomed them. *Zhob's* particular targets were the
participators in German business enterprises; they paid
"super-taxes." The "expropriations" were often indistin-

guishable from plain robbery. By a clever ruse worked out by Hersh Berlinski on January 30th, the safe in the *Judenrat* office was opened and 110,000 zlotys taken. All in all, in the first three months of 1943 about 10,000,000 zlotys were collected and sent to the "Aryan side" for the purchase of arms and ammunition.

Concomitant with its other activities and necessarily connected with them, in order to fortify its psychological position in the Ghetto, to instill in the Ghetto Jews the idea that no compromise would save them, and to make sure of its security, *Zhob* proceeded to implement its warnings of death to collaborators with the Nazis. The Gestapo agent Dr. Alfred Nassig, 75 years old, was killed in his apartment by Abraham Dreyer and Paul Schwartzstein. They found on him a six-page letter to his German superiors, detailing what he knew about the resistance movement and giving advice on how to suppress it. In February, Furstenberg, a member of the *Judenrat* and director of the terrible *Umschlagsplatz* area, was killed, together with Monyek Prozhanski and his son. On February 21st, in the office of the S.S. *Heeresunterkunfts-Verwaltung*, 38 Świentojerska Street, at 4:45 in the afternoon, Gestapo agents meeting there were set upon. Paul Wlodarski, Adek Weintraub, H. Mangel, and Lydia Radziejewska were killed; Leon Skosowski was badly wounded. The attacks on the collaborators spread fright in their ranks. Under protection of the Germans, some fled to the "Aryan side." Others were not able to leave in time to avoid execution. Among the latter were Hirschel, the manager of Hallman's factory, Fred Bobi, the boxer, "Pinya the Porter," and the infamous Gestapo informer known as Ele Malpe (Ele the Monkey).

The Germans did not demand reprisals for the assassina-

tions. They evidently thought it of no importance if the
Jews killed each other.

By the end of February Zhob had completed the reor-
ganization of its forces. There were 22 fighting units in all:
nine in the Central Ghetto, eight in the Productive Ghetto,
and five in the Brushmakers' Ghetto. Each group contained
from 20 to 30 young people, mostly between the ages of 18
and 25, with the arms noted above, as well as knives, clubs,
and bottles of acid. No formal titles of command existed in
the groups; comradely discipline prevailed. There were five
groups from Dror, four from Hashomer Hatzair, one each
from Akiba, Gordonia, the Bund, Poale Zion, Left Poale
Zion, Hanoar Hatzioni, and four from P.P.R. The identi-
fications did not mean that everyone in the group had the
same ideological background; rather, the names were derived from the political affiliations of the majority of the
group or its first organizers.

Mordecai Anielewicz remained the Commander-in-
Chief, and Isaac Zuckerman the Vice-Commander. The
commander of the Central Ghetto was Israel Kanal. Under
him were groups headed by Zechariah Artstein, Berl
Braude, Aaron Bruskin, Mordecai Grauvas, Leib Grusaltz,
David Hochberg, Henyek Zilberberg, Joseph Farber, Simon
Kaufman, and Leib Rotblatt.

The Brushmakers' district, commanded by Marek Edelman, had its headquarters in a bunker at the triangle of
Franciskańska, Wolowa, and Świentojerska Streets. The
groups were led by Hersh Berlinski (Left Poale Zion),
Yurek Blones (P.P.R.), Henoch Gutman (Dror), Yurek
Greenspan (P.P.R.), and Jacob Proszkier (Hanoar Hatzioni).

The Productive Ghetto forces were commanded by Eliezer Geller. Here in bunkers and in factories were the bases of groups led by Benjamin Wald (Dror), Joseph (also known as Solomon) Winogran (Hashomer Hatzair), Meyer Meyerowitz (Poale Zion), Jacob Feigenblat (Gordonia), David Nowodworski (Hashomer Hatzair), Hirsch Kawa (P.P.R.), Adolf Hirschhorn, Wolf Rozowski (Bund), Adam Schwartzfuchs (P.P.R.), and Isaac Blaustein (Dror).

A separate post was set up on Muranowska Square. Its leader was the teacher Elihu Gutkowski. Cooperating with it was the Jewish Military Union section led by Leib Rodal, comparatively well armed with 300 grenades, eight automatic revolvers, and one light and two heavy machine guns. As noted above, the Jewish Military Union also had groups operating in each of the Ghetto districts.

Another group, made up of porters, on Mila and adjacent streets, was commanded by Gottlieb, a Jewish officer in the Polish People's Army, an underground military body connected with the Polish Socialist Party. Through direct contact with Bundists outside the Ghetto he was able to smuggle in a quantity of weapons.

A few armed groups other than those named above and differing from the unorganized bands of the previous period were also in existence. These were the "wild ones," who boasted that they had more weapons than *Zhob* and who joined with, and then separated from, *Zhob* in various battles later on. The largest group was led by the porter known as "Moishe Bolshevik." Other groups were at Mellon's place on Wolowa Street and at Bernstein's on Franciskańska Street. Weapons were also secreted in a few bunkers by their inhabitants for self-defense.

Zhob worked out its general strategy. Recognizing that no uprising could possibly end in complete victory, it proposed to attack as strongly and as often as it could, to join other (Polish) resistance groups if feasible, to try to rescue as many Jews as was practical, and, in the final stages of the conflict, to withdraw and escape to join the partisan bands in the forests. *Zhob* figured that the narrow streets of the Ghetto would hinder the enemy's movements of artillery, tanks, and large military detachments. It felt street barricades would be useless. Attacks would have to be made on the Germans as they marched in to liquidate the Ghetto. To avoid such surprises as in January, guard-posts were set up in houses at the corners of the streets leading to the entrances to the Ghetto; provisions were made for prompt notification of any unusual activity on the part of the Nazis. After its initial attacks, *Zhob* planned to withdraw its forces to the underground labyrinth of bunkers and tunnels. These would be used as bases from which sorties would be made to harass the Germans while the mass of Jews would be evacuated to the "Aryan side." Diversionary actions would be the burning of German warehouses and factories. And when they felt their missions had been accomplished, the fighting groups would themselves withdraw completely and gradually make their way to the partisans nearby. The over-all plan was heartily endorsed by the People's Guards, who looked on Jewish resistance as part of the general Polish anti-Hitler movement.

The calling off of the January deportations had impressed the Poles deeply; German invulnerability was seen to be a myth. Acts of sabotage and attacks on Germans and their collaborators increased in number. The Left underground press brought forward the question, "If the Jews can do it, why not you?" The Germans feared that the rest of Warsaw would follow the example of the Jews and a general uprising would develop. To forestall such a contingency, hundreds of Polish workers were arrested in January in mass raids on the ground of subversive activity. Naturally, such retaliation had its effect on the Poles' attitude toward the Jews: some became more anxious to help them; others blamed them for bringing the wrath of the Germans down on Polish heads. At a meeting of the Council for Aid to the Jews, the representative of the Polish government-in-exile advised against any armed attacks as a means of helping the Jews: "Reprisals would be inevitable. Such acts are forbidden by London."

The Germans were not at all passive regarding the Jewish question during this entire period. The rulers of Warsaw had Himmler's directives hanging over their heads, but the unrest in the city made them hesitate to return to the use of force so soon. They therefore used the ever-obliging *Judenrat* once more. On January 27th the *Judenrat* ordered that all Jews between the ages of 16 and 45 were to appear for registration and work assignments. Fooled once by "registrations," the Jews would not be fooled again. Only a handful reported. *Zhob* hurriedly put out a leaflet advising against registering, saying also, "No other hope lies but in fighting. Once you are in the wagon for Treblinka, you are lost! Make every house a fortress!"

The registration ruse having been unsuccessful, the Nazis now tried a new tactic—"peaceful methods." The industrialist Walter C. Toebbens was appointed head of a commission to get the Jews out of Warsaw "peacefully."

The "peaceful methods" were only a variant on the old "selections." Toebbens announced that the Warsaw Jews were to be relieved of nonproductive elements, who were to be resettled. Thus the productive workers would have more to eat and better living conditions. Meanwhile, the factory workers themselves were urged to volunteer for work in the S.S. labor camps at Trawniki and Poniatow. Factories would be dismantled and reassembled in those camps and the workers and their families would live in peace and quiet there. There was a hint that the non-volunteers would suffer the fate of the nonproductive. The volunteers would go to a veritable Garden of Eden, complete with baths, swimming pools, hospitals, schools, concert orchestras—and factories, of course—but making goods for the civilian population only, not for the German Army. Toebbens was assisted in his propaganda by the Jewish managers of several firms; among them were Jacob Hirshfeld (later assassinated for his collaboration with the Germans), Weinberg, and Glowinski. They asserted that they had inspected the camps at Trawniki and Poniatow and that Toebbens had not lied about them. In return for their cooperation they had been promised "iron letters," guarantees that their lives would be spared by the Nazis. A few factory managers from the Lublin area were also imported to support the story.

Zhob was ready. They beat up the Jewish managers from Lublin, terrorizing them so that they fled from the Ghetto. Leaflets with the slogan, "Trawniki and Poniatow mean Treblinka!" were broadcast. The Jews believed *Zhob*, not Toebbens, whose propaganda had overreached itself. He went ahead with his plans anyway. Hallman's woodworking shop was the first scheduled to be evacuated, but out of the thousand workers there only 25 answered the call to leave with their machines. The workers refused to let the machines be taken out. That same night a *Zhob* group under the direction of Joseph Winogran set fire to the building, destroying the machines. They also burned a row of houses on Nowolipie Street, used by Hallman as storage places for wood, boards, and finished furniture for export to the Reich. Ironically enough, among the incendiaries was Chaim Arbuz, the son of a former wealthy furniture manufacturer, and the factory he helped burn was one that had been confiscated from his father by the Nazis.

Toebbens' second attempt was a bit more successful. The machines from the Schultz and Schilling Brush Works were removed and taken in trucks to the *Umschlagsplatz* for loading on freight cars. There *Zhob* set the trucks afire, ruining the machines. Out of the 1600 workers, 250 showed up for transportation, but on the way to the trains many broke ranks and ran. Sixty were caught but were freed by an armed *Zhob* group that overpowered the 30 German guards.

Another phase of the "peaceful methods" was the use by the Germans of diversionary movements to expose and then eliminate the most active supporters of resistance. Ganzweich, the former chief of the "Thirteeners," a pseudo-philanthropic organization of the pre-July Ghetto that had served as a cover-up for Gestapo informants, suddenly reappeared in the Ghetto. He found new adherents who put out a paper, *Zhagiev* ("The Spark"), the supposed continuation of a journal that had ceased publication in May, 1942. The paper, after a series of inflammatory militant articles, called for a general demonstration before the *Judenrat* offices as a prelude to a spontaneous armed uprising. *Zhob* combatted *Zhagiev* vigorously, stressing its provocative nature. It went further. A member of *Zhob*, known only as Ignatz, shot one of its editors. Ganzweich then tried to start an Anti-Communist League but met with no success and soon disappeared from the scene.

Another attempt at confusion was seen in the activities of the agent-provocateur, Captain Lontzki, a former officer in the Polish Army. He set up an "Association of Free Jews," with the same aim of starting premature attacks on the Germans, who could then isolate and destroy the ringleaders. Both *Zhob* and the Jewish Military Union issued a circular, warning that the Association was a Gestapo front. Lontzki's group had some small successes in one or two shops, but the exposure effectively put the quietus on its further activity.

Zhob began to test its strength. Early in February, two German Factory Police officers were killed. On February 11th, an S.S. man was killed and his Mauser gun taken. On February 16th, two German militiamen were killed by a group led by the Pole, Captain Ketling; their uniforms and guns were taken.

Himmler was not at all happy with the way things were going in the Ghetto. On February 16th, he wrote to Higher S.S. and Police Leader Krueger:

> For security reasons I hereby order the destruction of the Warsaw Ghetto. . . . On execution of these orders you will salvage the material to be found there and those buildings which are still serviceable.
>
> The destruction of the Ghetto [is] necessary. Otherwise it

is impossible to restore calm to Warsaw and to put an end to the criminality which will continue as long as the Ghetto exists.

Kindly furnish me with a detailed plan. . . . This district, now inhabited by fifty thousand subhumans, and which therefore could never be fit for use by Germans, must be absolutely razed to the ground. Warsaw, a city of a million in population, a dangerous center in a continual state of ferment and rebellion, must be absolutely reduced in size.

Oswald Pohl, the chief of the Economic Administration Headquarters, was ordered to take charge and make a full accounting of the goods and machinery, and Krueger of the people and houses.

Himmler's letter could not safely be ignored. "Peaceful methods" continued, but now they were augmented by a series of terroristic acts calculated to make the Jews realize that life in the Ghetto was unbearable, that they had better leave voluntarily for the S.S. camps. Soldiers and factory police ranged up and down the streets shooting at random. When the streets became totally deserted, soldiers would go into houses and amuse themselves by torturing the inhabitants or by trying out novel methods of murder.

Zhob struck back. On March 4th, 30 out of the 350 workers forcibly taken for deportation to Trawniki broke loose from their captors and took refuge in houses along the way. Retaken, they were confined in a temporary prison from which they were freed a short time later by a group from *Zhob*. On March 6th, an S.S. warehouse at 31 Nalewki Street was set afire by a group from the Jewish Military Union with the help of some workers there; the fire destroyed completely a stock of mattresses, bed linen,

and blankets destined for military hospitals. On March
13th, *Zhob* did away with two of the most notorious of the
German sadists. Three German factory policemen were attacked on Mila Street, near Zamenhof Street, while they
were indulging in their daily target practice—at Jews. One
was killed, one wounded, and one disarmed. Of the S.S.
men who came to their rescue, one was wounded. Similar
attacks on the factory police were made elsewhere. On
Muranowska Street a group of porters and smugglers killed
a Luftwaffe officer in the act of robbing a Jew. On Leszno
Street, two Germans and a Polish "blue" ("blue police"—
from the color of their uniforms) were killed.

The Germans promptly responded to these assaults on
their personnel. Obersturmführer Brandt undertook to
"pacify" the Ghetto. The same day, from 2:00 to 4:00
P.M., his detachments collected victims. They dragged out
200 Jews, including 14 children, from the houses on Mila
Street, between Zamenhof and Nalewki Streets, and killed
them then and there.

The attacks on the Germans ceased. *Zhob* felt that the
cost was too great, that such sporadic forays were actually
defeating one of their purposes—the saving of Jewish lives.
It redoubled its efforts to combat Toebbens' propaganda
which, by dint of repetition and the terror in the Ghetto,
began to have some effect on the workers. It started by
posting large placards repeating the warning that voluntary
deportation was suicide.

Toebbens answered these posters with an "open letter to
the Jewish workers in the armaments industry in the Jewish
quarter," printed and prominently displayed in all the
shops. Toebbens said:

I categorically state that no forcible deportations will be made. Neither Herr Schultz nor I have been constrained by threats to take part in any such action. Those who went out in the last transport were *not* put to death.

It is too bad that the armaments workers at Schultz's did not follow my well-meant advice. I regret also that I had to remove one factory to take advantage of transport facilities. Those who are already at Trawniki are to have their baggage sent there at once.

The fact that those who went from the factory on Prosta Street [the Toebbens shop in the Small Ghetto] did not know where they were going, actually to Poniatow, proves that secrecy, they being armament workers, was necessary. People have already returned with trucks to take out the rest of the machines. A Jew is in charge of the baggage not yet forwarded. Engineer Lipschitz will give you information any time about the whole business. . . .

Jewish armaments workers! Don't believe those who want to mislead you. They only want to excite you, and the end will be disastrous. The bunkers offer no security; neither does life in the Aryan district. Insecurity and idleness only lower the morale of people accustomed to work. I ask you— why do rich Jews from the Aryan side come to me of their own free will and ask me for jobs? They have enough money to live on but they can't stand inactivity. I give you my most heartfelt advice—go to Trawniki, go to Poniatow, because there at least you will have a chance to live and survive the war. The leaders of *Zhob* cannot help you. They give you false promises. They'll sell you places for cash in the bunkers and then they'll drive you out and leave you to your fate. Trust only the German business leaders who will carry on production with your help at Poniatow and Trawniki. Take your wives and children with you—we'll take care of them!

The appeal brought inconsequential results. Toebbens then asked the *Judenrat* to arrange a conference with the leaders of *Zhob* so that he could convince them of his sincerity. *Zhob* rejected the outstretched hand. In response to Toebbens' order to call such a conference anyway, Marek Lichtenbaum, the president of the *Judenrat*, said flatly, "I have no longer any power in the Ghetto. Another force rules now."

During March *Zhob* intensified its activities, procuring weapons, training cadres, and freeing arrested workers, and added to them by making a levy in the Ghetto for money for the support of children on the "Aryan side." The smuggling of children to safety had been going on steadily. Its tempo now increased; there was need for financial aid to support the children in the convents and Catholic orphan asylums and in the homes of the Polish people who had taken them in as supposedly orphaned relatives.

Also during March the London radio broadcast for the first time the story of the January resistance. The broadcast both heartened the Jews in their hope that now the Allies would come to their rescue and discouraged them because it had taken so long to convince their Polish compatriots abroad that they were in desperate straits, fighting for their lives. The first viewpoint was communicated in a letter from a Jewish youth group to an "Aryan" youth group; it brimmed with enthusiasm and expressions of good will, full of confidence. The second was shown in the bitter title of a mimeographed Revisionist paper, *"Morituri te salutant Judea!"* The Revisionists had reason for their feelings. Major Januszewski, of the *Armja Krajowa*, told Isaac Zuckerman that he would not aid the Jew-Communist, that if they went out anyway in actual combat, he would fight against them.

Extermination was quickly reaching the top of the agenda. Von Sammern-Frankenegg, in consultation with Governor-General Frank, drew up plans for the evacuation of all Jews and their workshops from Warsaw. The Nazis wanted to profit a while longer from Jewish slave labor and to realize the value of the raw materials and machinery in the Ghetto. They therefore had to use methods which would not be overdestructive and yet would be thorough. Von Sammern-Frankenegg's plan was to (1) ring the Ghetto completely with machine gun emplacements all around the walls, (2) break off all tramway connections in the streets near the Ghetto, (3) extend street raids for forced deportations, (4) concentrate armed forces on Zamenhof Street, then spread out in all directions, and clear out the Ghetto by force, (5) continue to use Toebbens and Schultz to persuade the workers to leave en masse without causing any trouble, (6) organize workers in large groups to leave their places and move out on the pretext that they were being transferred to other parts of the Ghetto. A strong force would be necessary, von Sammern-Frankenegg said. Authority was given to him to use whatever troops he needed. Accordingly, by April 16th the following forces were placed under his command:

Waffen-S.S.: S.S. Panzer-Grenadier Battalion #3,
       Warsaw, 4/400 (4 officers and 400 men)
       S.S. Cavalry Battalion, Warsaw, 5/381
Ordnungs-Police: S.S. Police, 1st and 3rd Battalions,
       22nd Regiment, 6/128
       Technical Force 1/6

   Polish Police 4/363
   Polish Fire Brigade 166
   Security Police 3/32
 Army units: Light artillery battery 2/22
   Sappers' group from Railway Panzer Section 2/42
   14th Sappers' unit 1/34
Askaren [Collaborators—Letts, Lithuanians, Ukrainians]
   from Trawniki: 2/335

Von Sammern-Frankenegg was assured of the fullest co-operation from Dr. Hahn, Ludwig Fischer, the Governor of Warsaw, and Lieutenant-General Rossim, the military commander of the Warsaw district. To make sure that Berlin would be satisfied, Krueger called a 48-year-old career Nazi, the General of Police and Brigade Leader S.S. Jürgen Stroop from Lwow to take over operations at his discretion.

An additional 7000 S.S. men, police, and militiamen were assigned to the general area of Warsaw to forestall any attempt by the Jews to break out and to hide in the "Aryan" sections and to intimidate the Polish population, should they be aroused by the liquidations.

It was estimated that the entire operation would be over in three days, the Jews cleared out of Warsaw, and Himmler well satisfied.

CHAPTER VIII

The Uprising: April 19 Through May 16, 1943

AT 2:30 A.M. on Monday, April 19, 1943, the beginning of Passover, the *Zhob* outposts reported unusual stirrings amongst the Germans. By 3:00 A.M., German guards, placed every 25 meters, completely surrounded the Ghetto walls, with machine guns set up at some stations. German reconnaissance parties roamed through the unoccupied parts of the Ghetto. Hauptsturmführer Brandt drove around in a black automobile, checking up on his men. By this time *Zhob* had sent out special patrols to warn the Ghetto that an "action" was imminent, that everyone should stay hidden. Placards saying, "Let us die with honor!" "Fight! Women and children to the bunkers!" were put up. Over one wall a sheet was flung painted with slogans calling on the Poles to fight in solidarity with the Jews. By 4:00 A.M., all the *Zhob* units were alerted and in their previously planned positions, with the main concentration points at the corner of Nalewki and Gensia Streets, on Zamenhof Street, and at the corner of Muranowska and Nalewki Streets.

At 6:00 A.M., German troops (16 officers and 850 men)

entered the Ghetto through the gate on Nalewki Street.
They divided into two columns; one proceeded along
Nalewki Street to empty the houses and collect the Jews for
deportation; the other, motorized, went along Zamenhof
Street, the trucks with infantrymen being preceded by
motorcycles, two tanks and an armored car, and followed
by an ambulance. Von Sammern-Frankenegg personally
led the operation, accompanied by Obersturmführer Bel-
wid, Hauptsturmführer Plenck, Police-Major Steinhagel,
Police-Captain Zisenis, Chief of Security Police Dr. Hahn,
and Chief-of-Staff Jesuiter. The commander of the Trawniki camp, Bartoschka, was also present.

Zhob was ready. It had planned to ambush the Germans
at the corner of Zamenhof and Mila Streets. Four groups
were assigned to this mission, with reserves in readiness;
they were armed with guns, grenades, and Molotov cocktails. They fired on the trucks from the house at 37 Zamenhof Street. The tanks pushed on but fell into the trap laid
for them. One was immediately enveloped in flames; the
other backed up and fled. The column broke up, the soldiers running to hide in the doorways of shops and houses
before making a disorganized retreat. Only one Jewish
fighter was lost, but twelve Germans were killed and many
wounded.

Meanwhile, the other column had also been fired on.
From the windows, balconies, and roofs of 2 Gensia Street,
at the corner of Nalewki, as well as from 31, 33, 35 and 37
Nalewki Street, and from Brauer's factory at the corner of
Nalewki and Franciskańska Streets, groups led by Zechariah Artstein, Henyek Zilberberg, and Leib Rotblatt,
armed with Molotov cocktails, grenades, a couple of rifles,

and the sole machine gun *Zhob* possessed, started the attack. The Germans had marched in singing cheerfully. Surprised by the sudden assault, they stampeded from the
street, leaving their dead and wounded behind. The Jews
swarmed out of the buildings and followed them, firing
constantly. Von Sammern-Frankenegg quickly sent reinforcements, but the counterattack was feeble. The Germans stood close to the walls, directing their fire at anyone
who exposed himself in the houses opposite. Two hours of
desultory shooting elapsed until the Germans retreated
slowly. The Jews again came out of the buildings, dancing
with joy as they despoiled the bodies lying in the street of
uniforms, helmets, and weapons.

The German commander was overwhelmed. He hurriedly left the Ghetto to call on General Stroop in his hotel.
Distraught, he told Stroop, "In the Ghetto all is lost. We're
no longer there. We can't get in. We have dead and
wounded." He wanted to telephone Krakow for air and
heavy artillery reinforcements. Stroop calmed him down,
made a few sarcastic remarks, and formally took over the
direction of the action.

Half an hour later, Stroop came into the Ghetto. To
embolden his frightened soldiers, he sat down on a bench
under a tree in front of the *Judenrat* offices and gave orders
from there. He organized his staff on the spot and called on
the Reichswehr for help. His example inspirited his men;
they admired his courage in staying at his place despite the
fact that twice bullets barely missed him. Using light artillery, he dislodged the fighters from 29 Zamenhof Street,
opposite.

By noon Stroop had regained control of the main artery

of the Ghetto by winning the corner of Gensia, Zamenhof
and Niska Streets. Troops converged from all sides on this
section, going single file, clinging to the shelter of the walls.
Tanks again came into the Ghetto. To prevent the Jews
from escaping from the area, the Germans hastily put up a
barricade made of mattresses, but the Jews, using Molotov
cocktails, set them afire. Their ammunition gone, the Jewish fighters gave up their positions in the houses and withdrew over the roofs. The Germans promptly took the spots
vacated by the Jews at 12 and 14 Gensia Street, good positions from which they could fire at their opponents on the
roof at 37 Nalewki Street. The latter were forced to pull
back to a cellar on Gensia Street. On the way they set fire
to the *Werterfassung*, the storehouse for stolen Jewish
goods. One of the commanders, Henyek Zilberberg, fell in
this fight.

Vexed by his setbacks, Stroop took a gruesome revenge.
The hospital was located at 6 Gensia Street. He ordered all
the patients killed and the hospital personnel removed. For-
tunately, some of the patients, nurses, and doctors were well-
hidden in a bunker under the sub-basement and so were
temporarily saved.

About this same time, a group of the Jewish Military
Union, led by Paul Frenkel, at the corner of Nalewki Street
and Muranowska Place, inveigled several *Askaren* into a
house, killing all but one. They kept up their harassment of
the Germans by shooting from that house throughout the
day; their attacks and the blue-and-white (Zionist) and red-
and-white (Polish) flags fluttering from the roof-top in-
furiated Stroop. He gave orders that the group must be
wiped out by the next day.

At 4:00 P.M., flame-throwers began to be used to dislodge the Jewish fighters from their positions, driving them to cellars, bunkers, attics, and sewers. Stroop's men pursued them vigorously. He ordered the sewers flooded, but the Jews succeeded in temporarily shutting off the water connections. Only 200 Jews were captured; many more were killed. In the indiscriminate shooting, about 200 Poles working under German orders in various parts of the Ghetto were also killed. Stroop counted only twelve dead Germans, obviously bad arithmetic, judging from other reports and from his subsequent actions.

Resistance was put up in other places: at the Transavia factory, by a group of porters on Niska, Dzika and Stawki Streets, and in the Oskaro factory, under the leadership of the gymnast, Felix Goldberg.

At 5:00 P.M., S.S. Leader Konrad was able to persuade a team of workers at the burning *Werterfassung* building to follow him for work elsewhere; he led them to the *Umschlagsplatz*. Out of the 4500 workers employed at Brauer's factory, the Germans were able to drag out only 380 by force. Nothing occurred in the Small Ghetto. Toebbens, anxious to save his machinery and merchandise, used his influence to stall off the use of force. He berated the Jews for their rebellious attitude after he had done them so many favors.

Sporadic fighting went on until darkness fell. At 8:00 P.M., Stroop ordered the withdrawal of his forces from the Ghetto and the strengthening of the cordon. During the night, the fighting Jews regrouped, held meetings, and planned the next day's action. One unit threw grenades at the wall on Bonifraterska Street, killing two guards and breaking part of the wall.

Outside the Ghetto the Jewish representatives were desperately trying to get help for the fighters. Isaac Zuckerman requested a personal meeting with Konar, the *Armja Krajowa* commandant in Warsaw. After much delay came the answer—"The Warsaw military salute the heroes of the Warsaw Ghetto who have shown that they can fight. I believe that a meeting is not expedient now." Zuckerman said, "I felt as though I had been stepped on." To his other requests for help came the cynical reply, rejected by *Zhob*, that help would be given the fighters so that they could escape to Wolin where they could take part in the anti-Red campaign. No response at all came from the delegates of the London Government-in-Exile when they were asked to send weapons immediately to the Ghetto, to give a prompt report to London about the uprising, to publish an appeal to the Polish people telling them what was happening and advising them to give the Jews help in every form.

The Germans were more concerned. The following morning, Tuesday, April 20th, Governor-General Frank sent a message marked "Urgent!" to Reichsminister Dr. Lammers in Berlin: "Yesterday we encountered a well organized armed resistance in the Warsaw Ghetto; to combat it we needed to use artillery."

At 6 A.M. of that day, a German column headed by a tank entered the Ghetto from the "Aryan" side of Leszno Street. It was immediately assailed from the windows of the third story of 76 Leszno Street by bombs, bullets, and Molotov cocktails; eight Germans were killed. The attackers, led by Eliezer Geller, had a well co-ordinated system of communications with other groups. They signalled those at the stations on Smocza Street to set off a previously laid mine under the feet of the Germans as they came through the street. The mine failed to explode but the tank was attacked with Molotov cocktails and burned. The Germans did not retire but fought back fiercely, killing so many Jews that out of the group of fifty-six only fourteen were left. The Jews had to withdraw to previously prepared positions at 61 and 63 Nowolipie Street. Stroop's men began the demolition of 74 Leszno (the Toebbens warehouse where Hirsch Kawa's group lay hidden) and the adjoining houses.

On the other side of the wall Poles also were fighting early in the morning. At 6:45 A.M. a mixed group from the P.P.R., Left Socialists, and the *Armja Krajowa* wiped out the machine gun emplacements on Nowiniarski Street, near the Brushmakers' Ghetto, killing four of the enemy and suffering no casualties themselves. Another group of the People's Guards, led by a Jew named Lerner, was only partially successful in an attack on the German post at the corner of Gensia and Okopowa Streets. During the confusion created by the fighting, an armed group of about a dozen Jews, led by the porter Yankel Rakower, managed to escape from the Ghetto through the Jewish cemetery, which bordered on that corner. They made their way to join a partisan brigade of the Polish People's Army.

Stroop had not forgotten the stubborn fighters in the block of houses on Muranowska Street. Here sixty men fought bitterly, beating back the attacks, making sorties, taking weapons from the enemy. They finally had to withdraw. S.S. Untersturmführer Dehmke was killed in the struggle over the flags. Stroop honored his dead comrade

by having one hundred captured Jews shot in reprisal.
Meanwhile part of the fighting group escaped to Nalewki
Street; another part went through the tunnel leading from 7
Muranowska Street to number 6 on the "Aryan" side of the
street. Here a Pole, Marian Kowalski, arranged for about
twenty of them to be driven inside hearses to a villa on
the outskirts of Warsaw where, two days later, they were
discovered by a German patrol party. Despite a fierce defense, they were all killed, among them Leib Rodal. The
others were concealed in the attic of the house on Muranowska Street, waiting for the contacts who were to lead
them to the woods, only to be betrayed to the Gestapo by
one of the tenants. A few escaped safely over the roof-tops;
the rest were captured after a short intense struggle.

Stroop had other booty that day. From a house on Mila
Street he took a red flag, which he proudly presented to his
guest of the day, Globocnik, the S.S.- and Police-Leader of
Lublin.

The headquarters of the Brushmakers' fighting groups
was at 34 Świentojerska Street, with an observation post at
3 Wolowa Street. Of the four thousand workers there, only
twenty-eight responded to the call for voluntary deportees.
At 3:00 P.M. three hundred German soldiers came to the
entrance of the district. A mine, laid two months previously
by Michael Klepfisch, was set off under their feet. They
ran, not returning until 5:00 P.M., when they were greeted
by grenades, Molotov cocktails, and the only two bombs
the fighters had. Again they left in disorder. From a safe
distance they started a heavy fire from three 2-cm. guns
and a 10-cm. howitzer. There was little response from the
Jews, already short of ammunition. The Germans sent out

men with white flags, asking for fifteen minutes cessation of firing so that they could remove their dead and wounded. (Stroop reported only two dead for the entire day's operation, an unlikely figure in view of the foregoing; a Polish trolley car worker reported counting almost 70 dead and wounded being carried out of the Ghetto from that area). *Zhob* refused, especially since, at that very moment, the houses nearby were being attacked by flame-throwers. The Germans pulled back. The Jewish fighters, joined by some civilians, also withdrew to the bunker at 30 Franciskańska Street, clashing on the way with German searching parties in the streets and on the roof-tops. Ammunition was limited; weapons were few—so few that those Jews who now wanted to join the fighters could not, because they had nothing to fight with. At 11:00 P.M. three scouts were sent out to make contact with other groups. While on their mission, in one of the attics they found the body of Michael Klepfisch, riddled with machine gun bullets.

Ludwig Landau, a Polish economist in Warsaw, who kept a diary during this period, says of April 20th:

> . . . Right now a war is raging all around us, a real war, with attacks and counter-attacks, fires flaring, tanks and cannon in action. It is a "Jewish War" of modern times in which events are taking place which require the pen of a Josephus. The impression created throughout the city is amazing. Feelings of sympathy are widespread. . . .

Sympathy was expressed not only in phrases but in action. At 7:00 P.M. Captain Joseph Przenny of the *Armja Krajowa* led a party against the German guards in one spot while another group nearby mined the Bonifraterska wall;

the dynamite made a large hole but did not break it down completely. At the same time, Jews attacked the guards from within the walls. Some Jews escaped during the action; others were caught by the Germans and promptly shot. Stroop commented in his report, "Today, again and again during the executions, the bandits collapsed, shouting, 'Long live Poland! Long live Moscow!'"

Not all the Poles were sympathetic. Dr. Adolf Berman and the Peasant Party leader Thaddeus Rek finally met with the delegate from London, Jan Jankowski. The latter said no arms would be given, but money would be forthcoming as charity to the Jews, provided none of it was given to the rebels.

On Wednesday, April 21st, trying to comply with the promise he had made to Stroop, Toebbens sent out an urgent notice to all the factories in the Ghetto. He ordered the Jewish workers to prepare for transportation, allowing them each 30 kilograms of personal property, and gave precise instructions as to where they were to gather and where they were to march. Only a skeleton force was to remain to supervise the removal of the machinery the next day. Stroop had as little confidence in Toebbens as had the Jews. During the previous night Stroop had directed a detachment of soldiers and *Askaren* to surround the buildings attached to the K. G. Schultz enterprises. Schultz himself called a meeting of the workers early in the morning and pleaded with them to go peacefully to the station for Poniatow. When the workers shouted, "Liar! Swindler!" Schultz threw up his hands and said that, alas! he could no longer help them and "for this you have to thank your co-religionists, the outlaws who have brought you to this pass by their underhanded dealing." As he finished his speech, Germans marched into the courtyard. The workers fled, but from the balconies all around, the group led by David Nowodworski threw grenades onto the Germans, killing a few of them. The Germans began to search each building, looking for hiding places. The fighters answered by setting fire to the storage rooms and by resisting every step of the way, fighting up the stairs until they could escape over the roofs. The Germans made no attempt to follow them.

About the same time, fighting was going on in the Brushmakers' section. The Germans set up a tight cordon around it armed with heavy machine guns, their aim being to prevent the Jews from escaping, especially the fighting groups. The Germans set fires in various buildings, hoping thus to force the Jews out for easy capture. They were unsuccessful. Seven fighter groups escaped, together with many civilians, and made their way to the well-equipped bunker at the Jewish Relief Office. A group known as "The Hammerers," made up of tinsmiths and locksmiths, ambushed a German detail at 28 and 30 Świentojerska Street, making them withdraw. The Teamsters' group at 4 Wolowa Street did the same thing. Dozens of Jews perished in the flames nevertheless. Stroop said, "Setting a house on fire drove out the Jews in hiding. Bunches of them—entire families—their clothes burning, jumped from the windows. . . . Steps were taken so that these Jews were liquidated at once." The walls in the area were stormed several times by Jews trying to break through, but murderous machine-gun fire drove them back.

Fighting went on elsewhere: at the corner of Nowolipie and Smocza Streets and in Wolinski and Pokorna Streets.

The bunkers were savagely attacked and as savagely defended, Stroop reported.

A Polish group, led by Edward Bonislawski, quartermaster in the People's Guards, tried to help the Jews by throwing weapons over the wall, but were caught in the act by a German patrol. In the ensuing conflict, Bonislawski was killed.

Stroop wanted to show that he would stand for no such nonsense as helping the Jews. On his orders, 150 Poles were taken from the Pawiak prison and shot on Zamenhof Street.

Landau noted in his diary,

> All of Warsaw has come to life with the news of the struggle of the Jews against the Germans. They call it the "Third Front". . . . The optimists claim that the Ghetto fighters can hold out for several weeks. In that case there are some who are ready to go to that front to fight the Germans. . . .

The Germans were well aware that a change in the attitude of the Poles boded no good for them. They countered any growth of sympathy for the Jews by intensifying their propaganda about the Katyn massacre of Polish officers "by Jew-Bolsheviks."

Zhob appealed again to the London delegates for arms and ammunition, but got no reply. Nor was the rest of the world greatly interested. The secret radio "Świt" near London broadcast the story of the Ghetto fighting; the broadcast was heard in Sweden and transmitted to New York the same day. Next day the newspaper *PM* printed the story. There was little impact.

During the night of April 21st, German planes dropped leaflets over the Ghetto, calling on the Jews to stop fighting and to report for transportation. At the same time, Stroop reinforced his patrols in the "deserted areas," where hundreds of Jews, hidden in the supposedly already evacuated houses, were found. The patrols had no easy going; the Jewish fighters used their knowledge of the Ghetto to harass them constantly. The Jews welcomed the darkness; it concealed their movements and gave them a respite in which to regroup their units and move their positions.

The three days estimated by Stroop as sufficient to clear out the Ghetto had passed. His frontal attacks having been unsuccessful, Stroop now ordered the burning of houses and a more intensive search of buildings, block by block. The Jewish sentries on roofs and in attics were able to warn some of the civilian population in time. They led large crowds from roof to roof over plank bridges from doomed hiding places to better ones. But the fires on Świentojerska, Franciskańska, Wolowa, Nalewki, and Zamenhof Streets proved that Stroop's new tactic worked. Hundreds of Jews were burned to death; hundreds more, fleeing from the heat and smoke and flames attacking their bunkers, were captured. Others found asylum in the sewers. Stroop ordered all the manholes to be closed, but in the confusion many were overlooked and Jews escaped through them. He then ordered gas bombs to be thrown into the sewer openings and poured liquid creosote into them.

The Jewish fighting groups roamed through the Ghetto now, attacking the German search parties, mainly in the Central Ghetto. Many of the groups were caught and killed immediately. Others succeeded in diverting the Germans long enough to allow their Jewish captives to escape. Women, as Stroop noted, took a great part in every action.

Polish groups again tried to help the Jews. A saboteur band destroyed a bridge in the Eastern Railway Station and set freight cars afire in an effort to prevent the transportation of the Jews. Another band, led by Captain Ketling, working with Barczikowski's Democratic Party, attacked the guards at Bonifraterska Street, near Muranowska Square; under cover of the fighting, about a hundred Jews escaped through the holes in the wall to the "Aryan side," but only a few of them were able to elude the Gestapo there to submerge themselves in "Aryan" Warsaw.

Zhob sent a letter to its "Aryan side" committee:

We are well. Did you send food packages [weapons]? Remember eggs [grenades] and candies [bullets] and what's most needed [rifles]. . . . Let T. [Tuvia Sheingut] say prayers for the dead in the cemetery [let the cemetery be the contact point].

And the following day, Anielewicz, the commander-in-chief, sent a letter to Zuckerman on the "Aryan side" in which he said:

I have only one sentence fit for my feelings and those of my friends: Something happened far beyond our wildest dreams. The Germans fled from the Ghetto. . . .

Yesterday we received word that our comrades of the P.P.R. had attacked the Germans and that the radio "Świt" broadcast a wonderful bulletin about our defense. I felt deep satisfaction. We have lots of work ahead of us, but whatever has so far been done has been done well. . . .

The conditions under which the Jews are living are indescribable. Only a few will be able to hold out. Fate has

decided that all the rest will perish sooner or later. The die
has been cast. In a very narrow hiding place, our compan-
ions cannot even light a candle at night because of the lack
of oxygen. . . .

Be well, my friend. Perhaps we shall meet again. The
main thing is that the dream of my life came true. I was
fortunate enough to witness Jewish defense in the Ghetto in
all its greatness and glory.

Himmler was exceedingly annoyed at the slowness with
which the liquidation was proceeding. He sent a dispatch to
Stroop via Krueger telling him to get on with the job and
ordering the complete destruction of the Ghetto. Stroop
excused himself by saying that he was trying to save materials for the Reich by thoroughly cleaning out one factory
after another, but that he would speed things up by burning
down the entire Ghetto. His report for the day indicates his
vexation at the Jews for not letting themselves be taken:

The whole of the Ghetto has been divided into 24 districts
for the purpose of today's combing out. One reinforced
searching party, starting out at 7:00 A.M., was detailed to
each district, assignment to be carried out by 4:00 P.M.
Result—600 Jews and bandits forced out and captured, 20
killed; 48 bunkers, some quite elaborate, blown up; gas
masks also captured. . . .

The whole operation is rendered more difficult by the
cunning way the Jews and bandits act; for instance, we
found out that the hearses used to collect the corpses lying
around serve to bring living Jews to the Jewish cemetery and
thus they escape from the Ghetto. . . .

The day's work did not stop until 10:00 P.M.—a long
day for Stroop's men, who put aside their duty of remem-

bering Christ's Passion on this day, Good Friday.

The propaganda battle also went on. *Zhob's* call was widely distributed throughout Warsaw:

Poles, Brothers, Soldiers of Freedom! . . . this is a fight for your freedom and ours, for your and our communal and national self-respect! . . . Long live the brotherhood of arms and blood of Fighting Poland! . . . Long live liberty! Death to criminal, murdering occupiers!

Stroop also published a warning that the death penalty would be inflicted on anyone found without a valid pass in the former "Jewish Residential District." He repeated the warning of death to anyone who helped Jews to escape or hide. To show he was in earnest, he had an entire Polish family, found harboring a Jew, shot near Kazimierz Square. The P.P.R. Youth Division answered him by pasting posters all over Warsaw saying, "Help the Jews!" and by circulating a leaflet put out by its parent organizations:

Poles! . . . The bestial slaughter of the Jewish population demonstrates the true nature of Hitlerism. This is the fate which awaits you under Hitler's rule. By fighting the enemy, we'll spoil his plans. Long live the armed struggle of the whole Polish people! Long live the military alliance with the Soviet Union! Death to the German occupiers!

The *Judenrat* no longer having any function, the Germans got rid of it. S.S. men shot the members of the presidium held as hostages: the engineers Marek Lichtenbaum, Alfred Stolzman, Stanislas Szeroszewski, and Dr. Gustav Wielikowski. Their bodies were thrown into the sewers, already heavy with the corpses of Jews overcome there by gas and starvation. What was left of the Jewish police force was also killed that day in the Gestapo headquarters at 103 Zelazna Street.

The following day, April 24th, Stroop began the systematic destruction of the Ghetto. In his own words:

> I ordered every block set on fire, including the living quarters belonging to the armaments works. One factory after the other was systematically evacuated and subsequently destroyed by fire. The Jews then emerged from their hideouts and bunkers in almost every case. Not infrequently they stayed in the burning buildings until, because of the heat and the fear of being burned alive, they jumped down from the upper stories, after having thrown mattresses and other soft materials into the street to break their fall. With their bones broken, even then they still tried to crawl across the street into houses not yet set afire or only partially burning. Jews often changed their hiding places during the night by moving into the ruins of burnt-out buildings, taking refuge here until they were discovered by special searching parties. Their stay in the sewers also ceased to be pleasant. . . . It was often necessary to use smoke candles to drive them out. . . . Again and again we noted that the Jews and bandits preferred to go back into the flames rather than be caught by us. Again and again the Jews kept up their firing. . . .

In order to deceive the Jews into thinking that the operation was over, Stroop changed his mode of action. Instead of starting at dawn, he waited until 10:00 A.M., and the 24 military details did not come in from one end of the Ghetto but from the perimeter all at once. Heavy artillery was placed on Świentojerska and Bonifraterska Streets and on Krasinski and Muranowska Squares to aid in the demolition of the buildings.

A well-fortified building on Muranowska Square near
Niska Street was so fiercely attacked by the Germans that
the fighting group there was forced to retreat, taking with
them a number of civilians to join the group on Nalewki
Street. The mass bunkers at 29 Mila Street became unbearable due to the heat and smoke; groups led by Aaron
Bruskin and Leib Rotblatt organized the evacuation of the
civilians there to better bunkers at 9 Mila Street, using
armed advance and rear guards to keep the Germans from
seizing the Jews.

The Jews too used fire. They set in flames Pfeiffer and
Weigel's factory, the military stores of raw wool and finished goods, and the military conserve factory.

Conditions for the fighters became worse and worse.
There were now on the average fewer than ten persons in
each group. Food reserves were lost in the burning buildings. The heat in the bunkers made life there almost insup-
portable. *Zhob* turned from attack and defense to "partisan warfare." At night, dressed in German uniforms and
helmets, their feet wrapped in rags to silence their foot-
steps, groups came out to steal weapons and food and to
search out ways of evacuating the civilians from the burning Ghetto.

Stroop did not close the day's action until 1:45 A.M. of
the 25th. He reported that, not counting the Jews burned to
death or killed when their bunkers were dynamited, 1660
had been taken away, 1814 pulled out of hiding places, and
330 shot immediately.

Goebbels took note of the situation in Warsaw. On April
25th, his diary states:

The Ghetto is now under artillery fire. When such conditions exist in an occupied area, it certainly cannot be said to be pacified.

The anti-Semitic Endek publication, *Walka* ("Struggle"), in its Easter Sunday issue, also commented, but in a different vein: "The misery of the Jews has been earned a hundred times over."

Fighting continued. People coming from church complained that the smoke and ashes flying over the walls spoiled their Easter finery. The flames enveloping the Ghetto, the methodical German advance in each sector, broke up most of *Zhob's* co-ordinated activity. Each bunker became the site of individual actions, as at 5 and 7 Mila Streets. Sometimes the Jews made hopelessly futile attacks and desperate outbreaks, being willing to die rather than fall alive into the hands of the enemy. Reconnaissance details were sent out to check the likelihood of mass evacuations through the sewer system; most were killed by German patrols; others could not complete their mission.

Stroop reported at the end of the day:

A total of 1960 were caught alive. . . . 274 Jews were shot. As in the preceding days, an uncounted number of Jews were buried in blown-up bunkers, or burned. With this bag of Jews today, we have, in my opinion, caught the vast majority of the bandits and scum of the Ghetto. Intervening darkness prevented immediate liquidation. I am going to try to obtain a train for Treblinka tomorrow. Otherwise, liquidation will be carried out tomorrow. Today, too, armed resistance was repeatedly encountered. In one dugout, three pistols and some dynamite were captured. Furthermore, considerable amounts of paper money, foreign currency, gold coins, and jewelry were secured today. The Jews still have considerable property. Last night there was only the reflected glare of fire to be seen glowing over the former Ghetto; today it is one great sea of flames.

He also reported that, up to the time of this report, a total of 27,464 Jews had been captured, with only five German dead and fifty wounded. The last figures are quite incredible, especially since on April 18th he had already reported twelve dead. He was evidently anxious to minimize his losses. An underground Polish agent reported, from a reliable source, that up to this day the Germans had lost a total of 700 dead and wounded, 150 having been killed in the first two days of fighting. An unfriendly (to the Jews) report said this figure was exaggerated, the total being only 400.

The next day Stroop reported that "not one of the Jews caught remains in Warsaw; the scheduled transport to Treblinka had no success." He also complained because now he had to deal with "the toughest and strongest among the Jews and bandits."

One of the bunkers discovered on the 26th was that at 9 Mila Street, mentioned above. Direct attack being found unsuccessful, the Germans withdrew temporarily to let a Jewish informer try his luck at getting the fighters to come out. He called out to them that the Germans had promised not to shoot anyone who came out voluntarily. One German followed him to the bunker, to be promptly felled by a bullet. The Germans then used bombs, shattering the balcony above the bunker and tearing a large hole in its roof, allowing them then to drop grenades inside. The fighters, led by Leib Grusaltz, decided to make the best of a hope-less situation, and came out firing. Grusaltz was struck down immediately; some escaped; the others were killed after capture.

That same day, three of the Poale Zion leaders hidden on the "Aryan side" (Nathan Buchsbaum, Dr. Adolf Berman, and Dr. Emanuel Ringelblum) got a telegraphic message out to their comrades in London:

> With guns in hands, we fight for the life and honor of the remnant of the Jewish people. We need means to get weapons, to save the children, to support the fighters. Help is needed *now*. A martial greeting to the Jewish workers in Palestine and the whole world!

Zhob sent another appeal to the official Polish under-ground:

> We have been fighting for eight days. We have had much sympathy but no concrete help from the underground Polish forces. You promised diversionary actions and armed aid, but nothing has materialized so far. There has been no an-swer to all our appeals. Send armed help at once; arms and ammunition!

This letter was unanswered.

The fires spread; the fighting continued. So did the at-tempt to fool the Jews. Early on the morning of the 27th, the German director of the Schultz and Toebbens factories, so far untouched by Stroop, called on the workers for vol-untary evacuation; the vice-director, a Jew, swore that no one would be killed if he were willing to work. The time for the volunteers to leave the area was pushed up from 10:00 A.M. to 11:00, to noon, and then to 1:00 P.M. Only hand-

fuls left the security of the bunkers. Two Jewish fighters
suddenly appeared with drawn revolvers; everyone fled. A
short sharp battle broke out between the fighters and the
encircling Germans; both fighters were killed. Fires were
started by the Germans in the building complex. Some of
the workers, unable to stand the suffocating smoke, sur-
rendered and were led out by S.S. men. Others, those at 76
and 78 Leszno Street in the K. G. Schultz warehouses, defended their bunkers so vigorously that Stroop had to send
reinforcements. The workers there had resolved to be killed
rather than surrender. They were killed.

Stroop continued his step-by-step destruction, utilizing
the services of Jewish informers promised their lives for
information about the sites of bunkers; 39, 40 and 41
Nowolipki Street, well-armed bunkers, were so betrayed.
Forty-one was blown up; 40, given an ultimatum to surrender, answered with bullets until the supply for the three
guns they had ran out. With the cessation of firing the
Germans entered the bunker only to find the bodies of the
fighters—they had all taken potassium cyanide. At 67 and
69 Nowolipie Street, other bunkers were opened, but without losses by the Nazis. Stroop ordered the bunkers to be
flooded. That at 74 Leszno became untenable; the fighting
group, led by Hirsch Kawa, tried to force its way past the
Germans; their leader was killed and only a handful were
successful in reaching other bunkers. At 4:00 P.M., a large
block of buildings was set afire on Niska Street, but fighting
continued to the bitter end.

One joint attack took place, the battle lasting until 9:00
P.M. Outside the walls at Muranowska Street, 120 men
belonging to Barczikowski's Democratic Party attacked the

Germans while a group from the Jewish Military Union stormed the walls from the inside. Darkness caused the fighting to stop; both sides withdrew to lick their wounds.

At the end of the day S.S. men reported to Stroop that the sewers were being clogged by the great number of corpses floating in them.

By the 29th *Zhob* had to recognize that a change in tactics was necessary. Ammunition was running short, water and food supplies were at the vanishing point, fighting in the Ghetto was less and less effective. The time was at hand for evacuation into the forests. Zalman Friedrich and Simcha Rothauser were assigned to go to the "Aryan side" via the tunnel on Muranowska Street to arrange for temporary hiding places for the escaping Jews. Their mission was successful; the Polish Communists Stefan Sawicki and Wladislaw Gaik and the Socialists Anna Wanczalski and Stefan Pokropek set up hiding places until the Jews could be led to join the partisan bands in the forests. The group at 56 Leszno Street dug a tunnel connecting to a sewer from which Gaik led them to a manhole exit at the corner of Ogrodowa and Zelazna Streets. They remained in the sewer from 9:00 A.M. to 4:00 A.M. next day before it was safe to leave; they then were hidden in the attic at 29 Ogrodowa Street, the home of the veteran Polish anarchist, Richard Trefon. Now that the escape route was known, Regina Fuden and Solomon Baczinski turned back to lead others out; they were never heard of again. Nor was Leah Korn, who also went back to bring out several of her wounded comrades. The groups led by Meyer Meyerowitz and Benjamin Wald found another way out of the sewers only to find the exit surrounded by Germans, who killed them all in an unequal fight.

Stroop complained about the difficulties he was having. He said that the Hallman buildings, supposedly evacuated, still had 36 bunkers and

> . . . from them and from other hideouts and from the burning buildings 2359 Jews were taken, of whom 106 were killed in battle. . . . Some sewer exits were also dynamited. . . . Two exits found outside the Ghetto were made unusable by walling them up. . . . Jewish and Polish bandits closed up the bunkers from the outside, warning the Jews inside not to give any signs of life in any event, so that they could continue to live in the Ghetto. Some of the armaments factories are being evacuated very slowly. In several cases one gains the impression that this is done intentionally. . . .

His last remark undoubtedly refers to the foot-dragging attitude of the industrialists unwilling to see their goods and machinery destroyed.

His tedious job of "capturing bandits and subhumans" continued on the 30th. Although by this time great blocks of buildings had been completely burned out, Jews still remained in concealed bunkers two to three meters below street level. The bunkers could only be found, for the most part, on information given by already captured Jews. The known subterranean exits were blocked as much as was possible; one was so well defended that a heavy gun had to be used to dislodge the Jews and fill the opening with rubble. Stroop said of this day that the number of armed Jews seemed to be higher than heretofore. A group from the Jewish Military Union, led by Weinstock, succeeded in blowing up a German army magazine, a feat unnoted by

Landau, who sadly records for that day, "The Jewish battle is gradually ending. A few are still fighting, trying to force their way out of the Ghetto."

May Day, the international holiday of the working class, was celebrated in a special way by the resistance fighters. From the bunkers at 76 Leszno and 69 Nowolipie Streets, armed groups emerged to fight German patrols. At 74 Leszno Street, once more occupied by a fighting group, a formal meeting was held at the conclusion of the Radio Moscow broadcast heard on the hidden radio; the twelve men and five women, gasping in the stifling air, so short of oxygen that the candle flame went out, agreed that "it will be easier to die knowing that Hitler is doomed." From 47 Nalewki Street, Jews disguised in German uniforms made their way unnoticed until they were in a position to attack a German patrol; their ammunition exhausted, they fled, hiding in the ruined buildings until they could make their way to 18 Mila Street, now the headquarters of *Zhob*. In the bunker at 30 Franciskańska Street, where there were about 100 people, mostly from the intelligentsia (including the non-party diarist Samuel Winter), the Bundists there led a short meeting ended by the singing of the "Internationale," after which several groups of fighters left the relative safety of the bunker to harass German patrols.

The Germans were alarmed by the recrudescence of the fighting. They ordered the bombardment of the Ghetto and intensified their assaults, particularly on the bunkers at 74 and 76 Leszno Street. At 30 Franciskańska Street, their grenades were answered by a hail of bullets and, as they pressed their attack, they were themselves set upon by a group from the rear, forcing a quick retreat until the next day when, reinforced, they resumed the attempt to open the bunker. In other areas the Germans had better success, but Stroop grumbled that "not a single Jew gave himself up voluntarily after his bunker had been opened." Many Jews were pulled out of sewer openings. Stroop noted with exasperation this example of Jewish *chutzpah:* An explosive charge was placed at a sewer opening; a Jew crawled out, removed the detonating mechanism, and crawled back into the sewer with the explosive.

A "wild" group set fire to a German storehouse on Gensia Street. At the very *Umschlagsplatz,* a Jew being shoved into a freight car turned and shot a police lieutenant. At the same place, ten unarmed Jews fought barehanded and succeeded in escaping transportation.

Polish opinion about the Ghetto fighting was still divided. *People's Struggle,* the Syndicalist organ, said, "Help is now impossible." *New Poland* made fun of the resistance: "Naturally, the uprising in the Ghetto will not be another Stalingrad, as the Jews hope." To which *New Roads* of the Democratic Party, indignantly replied, "Enough of this ill-meant irony! The Jews carry on the tradition of the Polish fighters for liberty."

Goebbels also had something to say:

Reports from the occupied areas contain no sensational news. The only noteworthy item is the exceedingly serious fight in Warsaw between the police and even a part of the *Wehrmacht* on the one hand and the rebellious Jews on the other. The Jews have actually succeeded in making a defensive position of the Ghetto. Heavy engagements are being fought there, which led even to the Jewish Supreme Command's issuance of daily communiqués. Of course, this fun

won't last very long. But it shows what is to be expected of
the Jews when they are in possession of arms. . . .

On May 2nd, the Transavia factory at 36 Stawki Street,
where airplane parts were reclaimed and renovated, and
the Wiszniewski factory at 54 Stawki Street, were cleaned
out by the Germans, but not without difficulty. Barricades
erected by the Jewish fighters slowed the advance of the
Germans, giving the inhabitants of the bunkers a chance to
escape. Ephraim Fondaminski, his wife Liba, and the engineers Wertheimer and Goldberg were among those who
broke through the encirclement to reach 18 Mila Street.

In the relatively quiet Small Ghetto, armed groups tried
to push their way out, but met with strong counterattack
from the Germans, anxious to make a good showing before
General Krueger, who had come from Krakow on a special
inspection tour of the "Ghetto Front."

The bunker at 30 Franciskańska Street was finally captured on May 3rd, after three days of fighting. The beloved
philanthropist Abraham Gepner was killed there, together
with about 50 others; the rest escaped to the surrounding
ruins or made their way to 18 Mila Street. The Germans
did not have an easy time. They used smoke bombs to force
the Jews out, and even outside, the Jews fought back.
Women threw grenades and fired pistols that had been hidden in their bloomers. Stroop therefore ordered that hence-
forth all captured Jews, male and female, would be forced
to strip in the search for weapons.

On May 4th, Stroop went ahead in earnest to destroy the
Productive Ghetto. The blocks of buildings belonging to the
various enterprises there were set afire. Four hundred and
fifty-six Jews came out to surrender, but many more waited

until the buildings were about to collapse before they tried
to escape across the burning roofs. Fighting on Leszno,
Karmelitzka, and Smocza Streets was continuous; again
and again the Germans used smoke bombs to drive the
defenders of the bunkers into the open. Combat went on
until midnight. At 2:00 A.M. it started again when a group
of fighters tried to reach the as-yet-undamaged Catholic
church on Leszno Street, used as an arsenal by the Jews.
During the night Stroop ordered additional patrols to seek
out and destroy any Jews still alive in the burned-out areas.
Nevertheless, small and large groups of Jews managed to
escape from the burning Ghetto over the walls and through
the sewers.

May 5th saw a continuation of the attacks on the bunkers. "Only by using strong explosive charges could we
break through an opening and wipe out the inhabitants,"
said Stroop. During the chaos of the previous few days
many Jews had taken refuge in one of Toebbens' warehouses on Prosta Street. Stroop cleared them out, 2850 in
all.

Next day was the same. The Jewish Military Union
bunker at 5 Karmelitzka Street was uncovered by the Germans and all the fighters killed. Stroop said about the
combing out of the Leszno area, "Although it was hardly to
be expected that any human being could still exist here, we
discovered quite a number of bunkers. The heat was intense in them. From these and others we dragged out 1553
Jews." The 356 Jews caught bearing arms were shot at
once "to prevent further German casualties." Stroop also
reported the wounding of two wall guards in connection
with a new development:

Jews who broke out of the Ghetto before seem to be returning now with the intention of assisting the Ghetto Jews with force of arms or liberating them. One such Jew who had escaped from the Lublin area was taken just outside the Ghetto wall. He was armed to the teeth with an .08 pistol, ample reserve ammunition, and two Polish "pineapple" hand grenades.

To prevent further infiltration of the Ghetto, the external cordon was extended in depth inside the Ghetto walls.

The Germans did not discriminate in their incendiarism. The church of the Blessed Virgin Mary on Leszno Street was burned, as was the Evangelical Hospital, and a row of historic buildings.

The Germans relied more and more on Jewish informers. Through them, the hide-out at 29 Ogrodowa Street, outside the Ghetto, was uncovered and the resistance group there, awaiting a chance to leave to join the partisans, was wiped out. The Germans were also helped by the Polish police, who "took pains to deliver . . . every Jew turning up in the city, the incentive being the bounties paid [one third of the possessions of the apprehended Jews]," Stroop noted.

Polish help to the Germans was to be expected. The radio appeal to the Polish people by General Sikorski, the Polish prime minister in London, to extend aid to the fighting Jews was countered by the Katyn propaganda and the underground reactionary press. "Great Poland," an Endek newspaper, said:

Some leftist journals, discussing the armed resistance in the Warsaw Ghetto, took on a pathetic tone, trying to make the Jews look like Polish national heroes. One of these rags had the nerve to proclaim, "The Warsaw Jews raised the flag first in the fight against the occupying forces." We must vigorously protest such applause. The fight of the Jews in the Ghetto has not the slightest relation to the Polish question. . . . There is neither heroism there nor danger. . . .

The *Armja Krajowa* paper, "Voice of Poland," said:

It happens that, as isolated Jews escape to the Polish side and seek shelter in the surrounding houses, Christians react with sympathy to their luckless neighbors. They forget their former vexations with the Jews and place their own lives in jeopardy by rescuing these people. But the *beau geste* must be mixed with common sense. The Jews fear the Germans more than death! When they are later caught, they show, in many cases, where they spent the night. As a result, for one Jew whole Polish families are killed . . .

Another journal, "Poland Lives," said:

The Warsaw Ghetto has been the scene of heavy fighting for several days. The Germans don't say much about these incidents because of the headache they're having. The Jews seem able to fight back the conquerors. It looks as though the S.S. and the police would rather fight defenseless merchants than armed Jews. These things don't concern us.

With such a background, it is surprising that acts of sabotage and assassinations of Germans on the streets of Warsaw still took place as gestures of solidarity with the Jews.

The Germans continued their relentless search for the hidden Jews. The Jews, forced to come out at night for air and to forage for food and water, were easy prey. About 30 to 50 were shot every night by the German patrols. Escapes through the sewers became more difficult, especially for large groups. One such, still surviving on Leszno Street, no longer having any ammunition, tried to get through the sewer that led from their bunker to the "Aryan" house at 71 Leszno Street; they had to remove stones and rubble blocking the exit; they were detected by German sound-apparatus; a gas bomb was thrown into the manhole; all the fighters and 150 civilians were killed. Another group was killed as it was climbing out of the manhole in Krasinski Park.

The Polish police reported that a number of Jews had been seen in scattered areas outside the Ghetto district; in two verified instances, on Tlomackie Street and on Grochowski Street, they attacked and killed S.S. men. "A crazy Jewess on Dluga Street shot dead two Germans and then fired wildly in all directions before she was disarmed."

Stroop made a scientific discovery on this day, May 7th.

Today we blew up a concrete building (on Smocza Street) which we had not been able to destroy by fire. In this operation, we learned that the blowing up of buildings is a very lengthy process, using up an enormous amount of explosives. The only and best way for wiping out the Jews, therefore, remains the setting of fires.

Zhob headquarters was situated at 18 Mila Street, in a bunker constructed in the ruins of three houses damaged in the 1939 bombings and badly deteriorated since that time. All that remained was a pile of bricks surrounded by walls one story high. In the lower part of a wall in the former courtyard a small gate led to a narrow tunnel seven to nine yards long, without room to turn around. The tunnel ended abruptly over a large, gaping hole. A slanting beam led down to the floor of this sub-cellar and thence to an empty corridor terminating at a solid wall with one hole in it large enough for a man to crawl through. Such was the entrance to the bunker.

The bunker itself consisted of a long and narrow corridor that connected on each side with adjoining cellars hollowed out of the very ground, big enough to accommodate a number of persons. Electric lighting, a well for fresh water, and a well-stocked kitchen testified to the care with which the bunker had been built. Each cellar, or rather large cave, had its own name, chosen with grisly humor: Treblinka, Poniatow, Majdanek, and so on—names of Nazi death camps. Each room could hold eight or ten people comfortably, but usually 30 or more were crowded together in the stifling heat. The bunker contained altogether 120 resistance fighters and about 300 civilians. It had originally belonged to "The Chumps," a gang of desperados and thieves whose chief was Samuel Asher, a man full of charity and compassion. He boasted that he had never turned away anyone who had come to the bunker seeking refuge. When *Zhob* decided to make 18 Mila Street its headquarters, he greeted them with respect: "Whatever is ours is yours. We are at your disposal." He ordered the gangsters to give *Zhob* full co-operation; they did so, acting as guides and messengers.

Before May 8th *Zhob* had come to the conclusion that all the fighters and as many civilians as possible had to leave the Ghetto. Its task there was finished. A heroic but useless death would serve no purpose. It would be better to escape and live to fight another day. Most of the sewer exits had been blocked by the Nazis by this time, but there were others. Blueprints of the entire Warsaw sewer system were in the hands of the *Armja Krajowa,* but not even the Bundist Dr. Leon Feiner was permitted to see them. A P.P.R. worker, Koszokowski, finally made contact with a municipal official who secretly gave him copies of the sewer system plans. A rescue expedition was made via the sewers to 18 Mila Street, but it arrived one day too late. By that time, the bunker had been discovered.

Probably relying on information gained from captured Jews, Stroop boasted on the 7th that he knew the location of the bunker of the "Party Directorate." On the 8th, the Germans blocked all the exits to the bunker and called on those inside to surrender. Some of the civilians, including the gangsters, came out voluntarily. The fighters and the others vowed to resist to the end. The Germans broke open the bunker from above and threw in grenades before trying to enter. The first German to go in was shot dead. The others quickly pulled back, continuing to throw their grenades inside. Meanwhile, a group of fighters had come through a tunnel from 22 Franciskańska Street, to which they returned, leading 14 of the fighters; the escape-way was then closed off by the Germans. Fighting went on in the bunker for two hours. The Germans then threw in suffocating bombs. That was the last straw for the harassed fighters. Many of them, wounded, quickly succumbed to the fumes, among them the Commander-in-Chief, Mordecai Anielewicz. Some decided to commit suicide rather than fall alive into the hands of the Germans. Only a handful, huddled in an alcove, remained alive, half-strangling in the smoke, until the delayed rescue expedition arrived next day.

Besides Anielewicz, among those who died at 18 Mila
Street were Myra Fuchrer, Ephraim Fondaminski (Liba, his
wife, had died shortly before the battle), Arieh Willner,
Berl Braude, Leib Rotblatt, with his mother and his Polish
wife Halinka. Because the bunker was the headquarters,
many others, among them the most active in *Zhob*, were
among the dead.

Up to now Stroop had written about the usefulness of
"smoke candles" to force Jews out of the bunkers, but in
the report for this day he says that innumerable Jews were
killed by the "smoke candles"—which were in all likelihood some form of suffocating gas, judging from the
graphic description of its effects given by Polish and Jewish
eyewitnesses.

By May 10th, Himmler became impatient with the failure to eliminate what he called "street fights" in the Warsaw Ghetto. He sent instructions to hurry up and use more
force if necessary for the rapid pacification of Warsaw.
Stroop acknowledged the instructions and went ahead with
the destruction of the Ghetto. He ordered the Transavia
factory to be burned down at once. More Jews were uncovered in their attempts to escape from the burning buildings and 42 bunkers were forcibly evacuated.

The same day outside the Ghetto walls two Jews "caught
carrying weapons" engaged Polish police in a desperate
one-sided battle on Bank Square before they were killed.
But by far the most exasperating event of the day to Stroop
was the escape from the sewers of a large group of fighters.
Zhob's emissaries, Zalman Friedrich and Simcha Rothauser, had arranged the rescue with the aid of underground Polish leftists. The fighters, 60 in all, including

Marek Edelman, starting at 5:00 A.M. from the garbage collectors' bunker at 22 Franciskańska Street, went from one end of the Ghetto to the other through the tortuous noisome sewers to the manhole opening on Prosta Street. Only 49 survived the journey; the others drowned or were suffocated by the foul air. They reached the exit at about 7:00 A.M. of the following day to find but one Polish comrade there. The Poles had called up a trucking concern for a truck to carry a load of wooden shoes, but the truck was late. Without food or water, the group clustered around the opening until the truck arrived. When it did, other Poles (from the People's Guards) put up a "Men at Work" screen around the manhole, terrorized the driver, and loaded 34 Jews on the truck, which promptly took off for the Lomianki woods and the partisans. The other 15 waited in a small side sewer for the second promised truck, which never arrived. By this time the Germans had been alerted. When the 15, impatient with their long wait, tried to climb out of the manhole, they were killed.

On May 11th, Stroop reported a shortage of "smoke candles" so that systematic combing out of the sewers was impossible. He also said that many Jews were still being found in bunkers (47) or hiding under the rubble of burned buildings. Next day, the Small Ghetto was carefully demolished by fire and dynamite.

The German annoyance at the pertinacity of the Jews was shown by the coming of an Extraordinary Commission from Krakow to investigate from where the Jews were getting their arms.

In London, Samuel (Arthur) Zygelboim, the official delegate of the Bund to the government-in-exile, committed suicide on May 12th, in a gesture of protest, leaving an open letter:

> ... The responsibility for this crime—the assassination of the Jewish population in Poland—falls above all on the murderers themselves, but also weighs heavily on all mankind, on the people and governments of the Allied nations, who have thus far made no attempt to put a stop to these murders. By their indifference to the killing of millions of helpless men, women, and children, these countries have become accomplices of the assassins. . . . Let my death be an energetic cry of protest against the passivity with which the world witnesses the extermination of the Jewish people and does nothing about it. . . . Perhaps my death will break down the indifference of those who—even at this late date—could save the Jews yet alive in Poland. . . . May the tiny handful who will survive out of the former several millions of Jews live to see, along with the Polish people, the liberation that will change Poland into a place of freedom with the justice of socialism! I believe that such a Poland will arise. . . .

The world paid no attention, and Stroop went right on with his job of combing out the Ghetto. The Soviet air raids of May 13th and 14th, well guided by the flames of the burning Ghetto, did not hold him back. His only complaint on the 13th was that the captured Jews refused to give him any information about other bunkers. As a result, the Germans had to use dogs and more scientific methods to find the bunkers. Their heavy approach, however, forewarned the Jews and led to heavy casualties on the side of the hunters. For example, a bunker at 3-5 Bonifraterska Street was found and besieged; Sarah Rosenbaum, the leader of the group, threw a grenade through the opening, severely wounding several Germans. The latter withdrew to bring up a light artillery gun. During the chaos of their withdrawal, the Jews escaped through a rear exit to Franciskańska Street. The same day a bakers' group in the courtyard of the big house at 6 Wolowa Street put up a fierce resistance, killing five Germans (Stroop reported that none of his men had been killed that day), and holding the others back long enough to allow some of the Jews to escape. One was caught, an elderly man named Bleiweis. He was ordered to tell where other Jews were hidden. He turned to the S.S. officer in charge and flung himself on him, shouting, "Murderer! Here's a Jew for you!" He was shot at once.

On the 14th, Stroop was annoyed by the attacks from the "Aryan side" on his men at the Ghetto walls and by the necessity of sending special raiding parties to drive "Aryan" guerrillas away from the roof-tops near the Ghetto. Perhaps his annoyance was increased by the presence of S.S. Gruppenführer and Lieutenant General of the Waffen-S.S. von Herff, Chief of the Personnel Division of the Reich Security Main Office, sent by Himmler to check up on how the operation was going. The Jews, death from Soviet bombs being the same to them as death at German hands, used the confusion created by the air raids as an opportunity to escape over the walls and through the gaps in them, particularly on Bonifraterska Street. Many of them succeeded in doing so—so many, in fact, that on the day following the Soviet air attack, Governor Fischer called on the Polish population to report to the police any hidden "Bolshevists" (Jewish and Polish resistance fighters).

The Ghetto was pretty well cleaned out, Stroop thought. On the 15th, only a few of the 29 bunkers uncovered were inhabited; the night before only six or seven Jews had been shot; during the day only 87 Jews were captured and 67 killed in armed combats, one of which he felt important enough to describe in detail. A special detachment searched the last block of buildings still intact and then demolished it. In the evening, the chapel, mortuary, and all the other buildings in the Jewish cemetery were dynamited or destroyed by fire.

The report on May 16th was brief:

> One hundred and eighty Jews and bandits and subhumans were destroyed. The former Jewish residential district no longer exists. The Big Ghetto Operation was terminated at 8:15 P.M. by the blowing up of the Warsaw Synagogue.

By the latter he meant the Great Synagogue on Tlomackie Street outside the Ghetto, a neo-Renaissance building erected in 1877.

The Big Operation scheduled to last three days had lasted a month.

In a carefully detailed report, Stroop gave the results of his work: 56,065 Jews were captured of whom 7000 were killed at once and 6929 at Treblinka, plus about five or six thousand more by being blown up or burned. Six hundred and thirty-one bunkers were destroyed. Booty consisted of seven Polish rifles, one Russian rifle, seven German rifles, 56 pistols of various calibres, several hundred hand grenades—Polish and homemade—several hundred incendiary bottles [Molotov cocktails], homemade detonators, bombs with fuses, large amounts of explosives and ammunition for weapons of all calibres, 1240 used military uniforms (some with medal ribbons—Iron Cross and East Medal), six hundred pairs of used trousers, parts of equipment, German steel helmets, 108 horses—four still in the Ghetto [hearses]—4,400,000 zlotys plus approximately five or six million more uncounted, $14,300 in paper and $9,200 in gold, large amounts of jewelry [rings, chains, watches, etc.]. With the exception of the few buildings used for administrative purposes, "the former Ghetto has been completely destroyed. Where dynamiting was not used, only fire walls remain standing. But the ruins still contain enormous amounts of bricks and unusable scrap material," said Stroop.

CHAPTER IX

The Rubble Fighters: May 16 to September, 1943

THERE was more than scrap material in the Ghetto. Embers still glowed in the former "Jewish residential district." Here and there a fire flickered up and quickly died down. The smell of burning hung like a pall everywhere. The spring breezes swirled the black ashes over the broken streets. The deathly silence was interrupted only now and then by the sounds of the German boots of the patrols and the occasional shots they fired at lurking figures in the ruins. For Jews still remained hidden in bunkers and in holes dug under the rubble. Some were armed, ready to pay with their lives if only they could kill a German when they were captured. Others, unarmed, buried themselves in their hiding places in the hope that eventually the Germans would depart and they would have a chance to escape to the "Aryan side."

The armed Jews were the remnants of *Zhob* fighters plus various other groups. There was no co-ordinated leadership, no formal contacts with the Polish underground, no fixed bases. They scrabbled in the ashes, returned to partly destroyed bunkers, to disguised lean-to shelters against the walls of burned-out buildings. They roamed from place to place in search of food and water, trying to get nearer and nearer to the Ghetto walls or to a sewer entrance so that they could flee from the giant graveyard. Disguised in German uniforms, they went out at night in short forays for revenge on the Germans.

The largest group was that of Simon Mellon, 25 persons in all, including a few *Zhob* members. Their initial arsenal consisted of ten revolvers of varying makes and calibres and eight grenades. Their first base was in a well-hidden bunker at 34 Swientojerska Street; later they removed to the fifth floor of the gutted house at 4 Wolowa Street. The stairs and lower floors were missing, so the Germans did not suspect that anyone could get up to the half-broken fifth floor. But the Jews managed—with a rope ladder. Another group was composed of *Zhob* fighters: amongst them Zechariah Artstein, Joseph Farber, and Isaac Blaustein. Another, in the Gensia Street area, was led by Kaplan (an alias, real name unknown); another, at 44 Mila Street, by Simon Kaufman.

The German patrols tried to ferret out the hidden Jews by cutting off water connections to the Ghetto wherever practicable and by putting noxious chemicals into other water sources; they poured gasoline over any food stores they found; they plugged up the manholes. As a sanitary measure they began to gather together the dead bodies and burn them in a makeshift crematorium on the site of the former People's School.

Armed resistance, no longer heavy, went on just the same. On May 19th, Mellon's group attacked a patrol in the ruins on Leszno Street, killing three Germans and despoil-

ing them of their weapons. The bunker at 44 Mila Street
was uncovered; the tiny band of fighters there fought so
fiercely that the Germans could subdue them only by using
gas bombs. On the 20th, short fights broke out on Nowolipie and Nowolipki Streets. On May 27th, Landau's diary
describes the spectacular fight that took place at 14
Miodowa Street, outside the old Ghetto. The previous night
a group of armed Jews had escaped from the Ghetto and
had hidden in the apartment of a Polish member of the
Underground Resistance. Betrayed by the *concierge* (later
shot by the People's Guards in retribution), they were
overcome by Polish and German militiamen after a sharp
struggle in which several Germans were killed.

An ironic tragedy took place the same day. A group
from *Zhob*, including some of those rescued from the
headquarters at 18 Mila Street, was concealed in a building
at 10 November Eleventh Street. The celluloid factory in
the same building caught fire. Three were burned to death;
one escaped, badly burned; one, unscathed, fled to a
nearby building, where a Polish woman kept him hidden
from the police in a chest. When she opened the chest to
tell him the coast was clear, she found him dead of a heart
attack.

On May 30th, the exposure of the bunkers at 37 and 38
Nalewki Street provoked a short battle; some Jews escaped,
but Blaustein and Farber were killed. Ten textile workers
out of twelve were cut down in their bunker on Okopowa
Street; the other two fled, finally joining Mellon's band. At
a meeting on May 31st, General Krueger expressed his dis-
satisfaction that so many attacks on Germans and "mur-
ders by Jews" were still going on.

In June the Germans complained again that their forces in the Ghetto were too small to combat the sneak attacks of the "Jew-Bolshevist bandits." The Polish police reported dryly that an unusual number of German functionaries were being killed by such attacks in the presumably cleaned-out Ghetto.

The sole aim of the fighters now was to get out of the Ghetto to the "Aryan side." The most likely area for escape was at Bonifraterska Street, where the wall had many holes and was partially down from the earlier battles. Zechariah Artstein led his group to 13 Bonifraterska Street and had almost succeeded in getting to the wall when he was surprised by a German patrol; in the ensuing fight, five Jews, including one young woman, and three Germans were killed. Artstein himself lost his life a few days later in another attempt to scale the walls. On June 3rd, the "hotel" (as they called it) at 4 Wolowa Street, now holding 150 Jews, was discovered; they fought desperately and had heavy losses but most of them succeeded in finally escaping into the surrounding ruins. It took them eleven more days before they could reach the bunker at 22 Franciskańska, where, they had learned, they would find a cache of arms. The bunker entrance was sealed by a pile of rubble that had to be painfully and silently removed; inside they found weapons and ammunition as well as putrefying corpses. Near Bonifraterska Street, the porters' group led by "Moishe Bolshevik" combined with another group from Muranowska Square to fight a police detail; most were killed but a few did escape to the "Aryan side." On June 19th, at 11 Grzybowska Street, since September 1942 no longer part of the inhabited Ghetto, a bunker containing ten former fighters was found and attacked by the Germans. In the all-day battle that followed, four Germans and seven Jews were killed; the others were overcome and shot, among them Paul Frenkel, from the Jewish Military Union.

The Gestapo again grumbled that during June the number of Germans killed was out of all proportion to the number of Jews liquidated.

Sporadic fights continued to occur up to the middle of July. The Germans resorted to their combing-out tactics—methodical search of the ruins of a building, then complete demolition of any part of it that had been left so that it would be level with the ground. In this way those few small fighting groups that were left were forced out into the open. Some were shot down, others fled into other ruins, and still others managed to reach the relative safety of the "Aryan side." Fights with the Germans took place on July 2nd, 3rd, 5th, and 7th, but no longer were of the same nature as the earlier battles: the Jews, swollen from hunger and dried up from thirst, were often too weak to throw the grenades they held in their hands. By July 15th, resistance was at an end.

A few Jews were still left in the Ghetto area. One by one, two by two, they died out or were fortunate enough to make their way to the "Aryan side," where some were befriended by humanitarian or leftist Poles. Most of the Jews so saved survived. In some cases, reactionary Poles or the blackmailers who made a specialty of preying on hidden Jews betrayed them to the Gestapo. Such a case was that of Tuvia Sheingut, one of the few surviving *Zhob* leaders, concealed in the apartment of the Left Socialist Stefan Pokropek; both were killed by the Gestapo.

One small group, Mellon's, lingered on in the Ghetto

ruins, unable to get out. It was not until September 23rd that they finally reached the broken wall at Bonifraterska Street. In the early evening, when the "Aryan side" was crowded with people, they frightened the wall guards by a barrage of grenades and got over the wall. The astonished Poles on the other side of the street did nothing to stop the Jews as, revolvers in hand, they disappeared into "Aryan" Warsaw.

Behind them they left a silent, deserted wasteland.

CHAPTER X

After September, 1943

THE resistance of the Warsaw Jews did not end with the death of the Ghetto.

A few Jews, hiding their identity, joined the *Armja Krajowa*. Most of those who wanted to be partisan fighters to continue the fight for revenge, for the honor of the Jewish people, for the liberation of Poland, cast in their lot with the People's Guards in the countryside around Warsaw. A separate unit, called sometimes "Ghetto Fighters" and sometimes "Anielewicz Men," was made up of Jews recognized as brave fighters in the guerrilla bands, often giving up their lives in battle. David Nowodworski died so, gun in hand against German soldiers. In August, 1943, Michael Rosenfeld and Adam Schwartzfuchs participated in the blowing up of troop trains and ammunition wagons. Both were killed in another battle with the Germans. Mordecai Grauvas lost his life in an internecine struggle with anti-Semitic Polish guerrillas. The same happened to another group in April, 1944.

Jews from Warsaw also took part in the uprisings at Treblinka on August 3, 1943, and in the resistance at Poniatow and Trawniki.

Jews played a great role in the general uprising in Warsaw in August, 1944. When the call to revolt came out, many Jews, living freely in Warsaw with forged documents, joined Polish groups and fought with them as Poles. Some who had belonged to *Zhob* met together to join up with the *Armja Ludowa* (People's Army); they were the only Jews who fought officially as a Jewish fighting force. Among them were Isaac Zuckerman, Tsivia Lubetkin, Solomon Grayek, Marek Edelman, and Joseph Sack. On August 3, 1944, Isaac Zuckerman, the head of *Zhob*, made an appeal over the radio to all Jews to join the fighting groups nearest them to drive the enemy from Polish soil. The Jews played a decisive part in the siege and taking of the main post office building on Napoleon Square. General Bor, in his report to the London government-in-exile, gave honorable mention to the many acts of Jewish heroism.

The revolt was crushed, and with it, for a time, the hopes of the Jews for deliverance from a cruel and relentless enemy.

Warsaw was finally liberated on January 17, 1945.

Postscript

So ends the tale of the Jewish Resistance in Warsaw.

It must be remembered that the final uprising in the Ghetto was the longest single sustained conflict in the history of all the resistance movements in occupied Europe. To accomplish that, under such unprecedented circumstances, is an achievement of which the Jews can be proud.

Glossary

ACTION Name given by the Germans to any operation regarding the Jews (deportation, shooting, etc.).

AGUDAH Religious (Orthodox) section of the Zionist movement.

AKIBA Zionist youth organization.

AMERICAN JOINT DISTRIBUTION COMMITTEE The main collecting and disbursing agency, founded in 1914, for funds from American Jews for relief and rehabilitation of overseas Jews.

BUND Familiar name of the General Jewish Labor Union of Poland founded in 1897. Socialist, anti-Zionist, anti-Communist in orientation, it was the largest organization of Jewish workers, with an extensive circle of subsidiary groups.

DROR Zionist youth organization, affiliated with Hechalutz.

ENDEK Acronym for National Democrats, a Polish political party with a reactionary and anti-Semitic program.

GENERAL ZIONIST Non-Socialist division of the Zionist movement.

GORDONIA Zionist youth group, affiliated with Poale Zion.

HANOAR HATZIONI Zionist youth group, affiliated with Hechalutz.

HASHOMER HATZAIR Zionist youth group, defense section of the Pioneer movement, with many sports clubs and training schools.

HECHALUTZ   Zionist Pioneer Youth movement, founded in 1905, emphasizing need for emigration and the building of agricultural settlements in Palestine.

HITACHDUT   Zionist youth group.

JUDENRAT   Council of Jews in the Ghetto appointed by the Germans for administrative purposes.

POALE ZION   Socialist Labor section of the Zionist movement.

REVISIONISTS   Followers of Vladimir Jabotinsky, advocates of non-cooperation with the British mandatory power in Palestine; strongly anti-Socialist.

SEJM   Polish Parliament.

UMSCHLAGSPLATZ   The square leading to the loading platforms in the freight yards, from which Jews were sent to death at Treblinka.

Bibliography

The following bibliography covers the main sources of the material used in this volume. A complete and annotated bibliography about the period of the Nazi occupation of Warsaw may be found in the *Guide to Jewish History under the Nazi Impact* by Dr. Jacob Robinson and Dr. Philip Friedman, New York, 1960.

BARKAI, MEYER (translator and editor). *The Fighting Ghettos*, New York, 1962

BORZYKOWSKI, TUVIA. *Tsvishn Falndike Vent*, Warsaw, 1949

FRIEDMAN, PHILIP (editor). *Martyrs and Fighters*, New York, 1954

GOLDKORN, DORKA. *Erinnerungen an den Aufstand im Warschauer Ghetto*, in *Im Feuer Vergangen*, Berlin, 1960

GOLDSTEIN, BERNARD. *The Stars Bear Witness*, New York, 1949

HILBERG, RAUL. *The Destruction of the European Jews*, Chicago, 1961

KARSKI, JAN. *Story of a Secret State*, Boston, 1944

MARK, BER. *Der Oifshtand in Varshever Ghetto*, Warsaw, 1955 (revised, 1963)

MARK, BERNARD. *Walka i Zaglad Warszawskiego Getta*, Warsaw, 1959

NEUSTADT, MELECH. *Hurbn un Oifshtand fun di Yidn in Varshe*, Tel Aviv, 1948

NIRENSTEIN, ALBERT. A *Tower from the Enemy*, New
    York, 1959
RINGELBLUM, EMANUEL (translator, Jacob Sloan). *Notes
    from the Warsaw Ghetto*, New York, 1958
SCHWARZ, LEO (editor). *The Root and the Bough*, New
    York, 1949
SEIDMAN, HILLEL. *Togbuch fun Varshever Ghetto*, Buenos
    Aires, 1947
STEMPELBERG, HENRYK (editor). *Menczestwo, Walka, i
    Zaglad Żydow w Polsce*, Warsaw, 1960
STROOP, JURGEN (translator, D. Dombrowska). *Report Con-
    cerning the Uprising in the Ghetto of Warsaw and the
    Liquidation of the Jewish Residential District*, Warsaw,
    1958
SZNER, ZVI (translator, I. M. Lask). *Extermination and Re-
    sistance: Historical Records and Source Material*, Haifa,
    1958
TANENBAUM, JOSEPH. *In Search of a Lost People*, New
    York, 1948
TURKOW, JONAS. *Azoi iz es geven*, Buenos Aires, 1948
———. *In Kamf farn Lebn*, Buenos Aires, 1949
WDOWINSKI, DAVID. *And We Were Not Saved*, New York,
    1963
WULF, JOSEF. *Vom Leben, Kampf, und Tod im Ghetto
    Warschau*, Bonn, 1958
YAD WASHEM STUDIES. Vol. I, 1957, and Vol. III, 1959,
    Tel Aviv

Map drawn by Catherine Coleman

UMSCHLA

POWAZKOWSKA
DZIKA
PL. PARYSOWSKI
CATHOLIC CEMETERY
STAWKI
NISKA
KOLTKA
MIŁA
SW. KINGI
JEWISH CEMETERY
OKOPOWA
OLINIANA
GĘSIA
ŁAWIA
DZIELNA
KACZA
MŁYNARSKA
KAROLKOWA
ŁAŹNIA
WRONIA
PL. KERCELEGO

The Warsaw Ghetto

Heavy line indicates original boundary

Shaded areas indicate sections remaining after
September, 1942

A—Central Ghetto
B—Productive Ghetto
C—Small Ghetto
D—Brushmakers' Ghetto